MENTAL HEALTH OF TEACHERS

MENTAL HEALTH OF TEACHERS

By

Surya Nath Prasad

Foreword By

Dr. John Paul Eddy

GYAN

Mental Health of Teachers

ISBN : 978-81-212-0323-4

First Published 1990, reprint 2015 in India by
Gyan Publishing House
23, Main Ansari Road, Daryaganj,
New Delhi - 110002
Phones : 23282060, 23261060
Fax : (011) 23285914
E-mail: books@gyanbooks.com
website: gyanbooks.com

Printed at : Sagar Color Scan, New Delhi.

Foreword

The mental health of teachers is one of the most important topics in the field of education in the world. If teachers have mental health problems, they will most certainly affect their students in negative and even in dangerous ways that might happen. Therefore, Dr. S.N. Prasad's timely book, *Mental Health of Teachers*, comes as a significant contribution to the profession of counselling and teaching. The influence of Dr. Carl Roger's "client-centered therapy", "Rogerian counselling" or "non-directive technique" is central to the thesis of this book. The counselling methods of Roger's are used in treating the maladjusted teacher-trainees who were in the experimental group of his research design that is the basis for his book.

Prasad provides an impressive scholarly documentation on the high incidence of teacher-trainee maladjustment in his volume. His goal for school teachers is to have them be as well-adjusted, satisfied and efficient as possible. It is Prasad's fundamental assumption that students need to have good mental health role models in their teachers so teachers need to be selected who possess those favourable characteristics and that these same teachers are helped throughout life to maintain these desirable traits. With these ideals in mind, Prasad dicovered in his review of the professional literature a lack and a gap in the research with an absence of studies on teacher maladjustment and how to help teachers through therapy become less maladjusted. Thus, the investigation of Prasad was directed at the identification of maladjustment of teacher-trainees and their therapy using the non-directive approach of Rogers (1942). In his study, Dr. Prasad identified 40 maladjusted teacher-trainees through the Neuroticism Scale Questionnaire of Scheier and Cattell (1961). He divided the 40 persons into two groups—experimental (therapy) and control (no-therapy). The results showed the experimental groups improved significantly during therapy and males improved more than their female counterparts. Significant improvement occurred in the follow-up experimental groups and no improvement was evident in either stage of the no-therapy group.

Prasad has contributed some excellent research using Roger's counselling methods that can help improve the mental health of teachers in training and teachers in general. Having studied under Roger's and having written articles on Roger's. I feel that Prasad's tome is valuable for professional counsellors and professional teachers world-wide. Consequently, I recommend this book for both counsellors and teachers. Moreover, this book should be read by all educators interested in how to improve the mental health of all teachers and educational personnel. Therefore, it is a must reading for administrators and the public that desires the best teachers in schools and colleges around the earth. This book should be on everyone's book shelf and in libraries everywhere because the planet called "space ship earth" needs teachers with the finest mental health personalities in a crazy world where sick persons would destroy the lives of students.

It is appropriate that Prasad, a counsellor, a professor-teacher, a scholar-researcher, and a leader in peace education (Editor of *Peace Education Journal* and past President of the International Association of Educators for World Peace) write this excellent book to help all humanity.

Prof. of Higher Education, Dr. John Paul Eddy
North Texas University,
Denton, Texas 76203, U.S.A.

Preface

The desire to pursue research in the area of psycho-diagnosis and psycho-therapy first came in mind, when I observed the mental patients being treated in Kashimano-Vigyanshala (Banaras Institute of Psychology) by its founder and honorary director Shri Lalji Ram Shukla, a celebrated teacher of Teachers' Training College, Banaras Hindu University. I used to assist him in his process of treating maladjusted youths and adults who mostly hailed from universities and colleges. They were students and teachers. I had opportunity to observe his process of diagnosing the maladjusted.

Due to getting initiation from him I enrolled myself as a research scholar 17 years ago on the theme 'Social Conditioning of Mental-illness' under the guidance of a world renowned psychiatrist and neurologist Dr. F. van Ree of Netherlands, then Visiting Professor at Kashi Vidyapith. But this study was left in the midway owing to sudden return of my guide Dr. Ree to his home country within a year of my work under him. This short span of my research work under him on the said problem left strong impression on my mind because I had the occasion to study sixty patients who visited him for their treatment.

When I joined the Janata College of Education, Chandrapur (Maharashta) in 1980, Dr. S.K. Jha, Principal of this College asked me about my interest of the area of research. I showed him my previous work. He advised me to register on a similar problem of teacher-trainees. This is the short story to arrive at the present problem of diagnosis of maladjustment of pupil-teachers and their therapy.

During my study I had always doubt in my mind whether persons involved in teaching can undertake to solve the problem of maladjustment of their students or not while it became clear with the mention of a teacher educator-therapist Shri Shukla who successfully played his role of both educator and therapist. I observed Dr. Jha also, who is a teacher-educator and psychologist, rehabilitating maladjusted children, adolescents and youths through his therapeutic process. But when I saw the book *Client-Centered Therapy* by C.R. Rogers my doubt was solved by reading Chapter 9 of this book in which Rogers (1951) asks,

> If. in therapy, it is possible to rely upon the capacity of the client to deal constructively with his life situation and if the therapist's aim is best directed towards releasing that capacity, then why not apply this hypothesis and this method in teaching ?

This was why Rogers had referred to "therapeutic attitudes on the part of the teacher" because Symonds (1949) also says, "The good teacher today minimizes his authority. He is interested in and accepts his pupils as individuals. He arranges to give the greater opportunities for expression..." And it was more clear when Felix (1955), Director, National Institute of Mental Health (USA) said,

> The promotion of mental health is not the responsibility alone of those who classify themselves as members of the mental health. The schools have long been recognized as influence second only to the home in determining the degree to which our citizens achieve that adult goal which the layman calls adequacy or happiness or self-sufficiency and which the psychiatrist calls maturity.

Maladjustment in teaching-community is a serious problem, because it affects learning and mental health of pupils. Even if the maladjusted teachers are identified in different studies and found their effects on teaching, the researches are not available on the rehabilitation of the maladjusted teachers or teacher-trainees. Hence there is a need for identification and therapy of maladjustment of teacher-trainees who are to be the full-fiedged teachers tomorrow.

The present study aims at psycho-diagnosis of maladjustment of pupil teachers through the Neuroticism Scale Questionnaire (The NSQ) of Scheier and Cattell (1961) but its Hindi Version by Kapoor and Kapoor (1974), and their therapy through non-directive approach of Rogers (1942). This book has been divided into six Chapters. Chapter 1 deals with mental health and education, effects of mental health of the teacher on the personality of his pupils, mental health of teachers in comparison to others and necessity of well-adjusted teachers in schools. Chapter 2 reviews the related Indian and foreign Studies. Chapter 3 deals with the conceptual framework of the study in which need and importance of the study, purposes of the study, hypotheses, delimitations and basic assumptions and definitions are described. Chapter 4 comprises procedure in which description of the test (The NSQ) used, description of therapy (Non-directive), preliminary try-out, and over-all design of the study are elaborated. Chapter 5 interprets and discusses the results on the basis of parallel group experimental design and analyses each case separately also. Lastly, Chapter 6 presents the summary and conclusions. In this Chapter practical implications are given to illustrate the use of the present study along with suggestions for further study.

The work embodied in this study is first of its kind as far as the knowledge of the present investigator goes. It fulfils a long felt need of psychodiagnosis of maladjustment of pupil-teachers and their therapy who may shape their thoughts after their own personality make-ups when they become full teachers. This study not only sought to identify maladjustment of pupil-teachers but also it covered therapy for their rehabilitation through the non-directive approach and tested their progress at post-and follow-up test points. This study can certainly be a guideline for further research in the area of mental health of teaching community, it is believed.

Acknowledgements

The researcher is greatly indebted to his learned Supervisor Dr. S.K. Jha, M.A. (Psychology), M.Ed., Fulbright Alumnus (USA), Principal, Janata College of Education, Chandrapur (Maharashtra) for his help, guidance and encouragement with his critical remarks so the thesis could come to its end. He expresses his gratitude to him also for extending assistance from the college in procuring the test material used in the study and for providing other research facilities.

The researcher feels a personal sense of gratitude for all the pupil-teachers who volunteered as subjects for the present study and feels sorry for the subjects of control group who were kept aloof from the therapy owing to the limitations of experimental design of the research.

The researcher is indebted also to the other researchers, authors, test constructors and its adaptors and therapy initiators whose researches and books are referred in the thesis and whose tests and techniques of therapy are used and also referred in the study and thesis.

The researcher would like to put on record his sincere thanks to Dr. Kamlakar Mishra, Reader, Department of Philosophy, B.H.U. who helped him by making available necessary books having issued on his own Library Card from his University, and also to his colleague Mr. B.P. Tripathi of his College who helped him in calculation of the data of machine.

The acknowledgements would be incomplete if he does not record the sacrifice of his son Master Maneeshi (who was at the age of 1½ years at the time of writing the thesis) and his wife Dr. Suman Shukla. Both of them helped him by keeping him free to complete the work in time.

He is grateful to the Nagpur University for giving permission to publish the thesis, and the N.C.E.R.T. (National Council of Educational Research and Training), New Delhi for sanctioning financial assistance for its publication.

He is thankful to Dr. John Paul Eddy, Professor of Higher Education, North Texas University, U.S.A. for writing the Foreword for the book.

Last but not least, he must thank M/S Gian Publishing House, New Delhi for bringing out the book in stipulated time.

Contents

List of Figures

List of Appendices

List of Tables

CHAPTER 1

Introduction and Background of the Study

Mental Health and Education

The concept of imparting mental health through education is not anything new. Long ago Patanjali, the author of *Yoga-Sutras*, indicated that the maintenance of physical and mental health is pre-requisite for self-development and self-realization. In the past problems pertaining to physical and mental health were tackled by different constituents of the society. But the situation is quite different today. Everybody expects in these days that the main objective of the educational Institutions must be in producing pupils who are physically robust, mentally alert, emotionally stable and culturally acceptable individuals. "Of the many challenges hurled at teachers," says Bernard (1952), "none transcends that of making the most of our rich human assets of keeping children and youth mentally, physically and spiritually sound. This is a challenge, and an opportunity offered by the mental hygiene Researches and Hypothesis".

The promotion of mental health is not at all restricted and

limited with the responsibility of those who classify themselves as members of the mental health professions, says Felix (1955), Director, National Institute of Mental Health, U.S.A. "The schools have been long recognized," he says, "as influence second only to the home in determining the degree to which our citizens achieve that adult goal which the layman calls adequacy or happiness or self-sufficiency and which the psychiatrist calls maturity." Scheier and Cattell (1961) are of the view that, the problem of neurosis is not the exclusive province of the clinician, but has to be considered by any practitioner concerned with selection and success in school, occupation, marriage, group relations, *etc.* However, this can be realized only when the guiding personnel (teachers) of the school themselves maintain good physical and mental health.

Effects of Mental Health of the Teacher on the Personality of Pupils

Playing a significant role in the development of the child's personality are the personalities of those with whom he or she comes in contact. One would believe that the close and extensive association experienced by teacher and pupil in classrooms would certainly influence in shaping the personality of the pupil concerned.

The teacher obviously is an important person in determining the ways his/her pupils are affected by and react to their work. To a considerable extent he/she can control the conditions of work, can also help so that the work is easier, and choose tasks, methods suitable for his pupils. He can very often help a youngster who is facing by problems. Teachers determine the environment of classes and the extent to which their activities are stimulating, refreshing or wearing. But to do all this teachers themselves ought to be free from fatigue and have a good mental hygiene. The problems of hygiene are chiefly concerned with the mental hygiene of teachers (Frierson, 1950 ; Kelicher, 1950 and Tyson, 1951). "Unless a teacher understands and practises good mental hygiene, he may become the victim of various emotion disturbing experiences," observes Crow and Crow (1956). Upon this Skinner (1958) comments, "It is extremely important that a teacher possesses adequate adjustment to the mental health hazards inherent in teaching." The occupational hazards of teaching include personality maladjustment, ill-health and a warped outlook on teaching and life.

Thus teacher's condition and personality unquestionably affect pupils. The teacher's condition is important because it affects teaching effectiveness and also his or her own happiness. The tense jitteriness of a tired or neurotic teacher is always unpleasant, and trials and tribulations of teaching tend to exaggerate such conditions. Teachers whose personalities are not conducive to pleasant and harmonious relations with the pupils are detrimental to the optimum growth of students. Inability to establish rapport with children or young students leads to ineffective learning situations, disciplinary problems and undesirable attitudes of teachers and pupils. An undesirable attitude of a pupil toward the teacher might indicate distinct probability that this attitude may lead towards his maladjustment.

Hence a sick, worn-out, spiritless, or unstable teacher tends to make his pupils spiritless, weary, unstable, inefficient and restive. A lack of balance of personality of the teacher gives rise to a condition of uncertainty and instability that is a deterrent to concentrated efforts and learning achievements of pupils. Teacher's fear, worry, unhappiness, self-pity, self-consciousness and emotional maladjustment tend to be reflected in their students' emotional reaction and their adjustment (Anderson and Brewer, 1945-46). Observation of Skinner (1958) is that "many teachers possess personality qualities that are serious handicaps in their work. They may be too sensitive to warranted criticism or they may become sarcastic and unfriendly in their school relations."

Mental Health of Teachers in Comparison to Others

The question arises whether teachers are more maladjusted than others in the society. At one time, the general folklore held teachers to be somewhat a neurotic lot. Semi-journalistic accounts (Shipley, 1961) painted a shocking picture of mental illness among teachers in the teaching profession. One survey (Smith and Hightower, 1948) of the psychic patients reveals that teachers are somewhat likely to be affected by diseases and ailments which are associated with neurotic trends (emotional maladjustments) than are persons in other occupational groups.

However, there are strong indications that extreme maladjustments are no more frequent among teachers than in population in general (Clark, 1950 ; Snyder, 1947). Ringness (1968) in one of his studies has indicated that teachers are no better and no worse in regard to mental health than the adult population taken in general. Fenton (1943) reported from his findings that 22.5 per cent of the 241 teachers employed therein could be classified as maladjusted. The medical examiner for the New York City schools stated that of the 37,000 teachers in that system, 4,500 were maladjusted, 1,500 seriously so (Altman, 1941). Another observer stated that in twelve years of schooling a child or student has 7-to-1 chance of having at least two maladjusted teachers (Townsend, 1933). A study of Ahuja (1975) indicated that 8 per cent of the 50 student-teachers were neurotics. Out of these 6 per cent had a high degree neuroticism. Bentz, Hollister and Edgerton (1971) have also found less mental disturbances among teachers than in general population. Table 1.1 shows their results on an assessment of mental health of teachers as compared with others.

TABLE 1.1

Emotional Adjustment of Teachers and other Groups

Group	Teachers	General Public	Community Leaders
Number of people in each group	379	1404	418
Average scores for* each Group	25.9	26.8	25.7*
Percentage of People with :			
Good Adjustment (Scores 20-26)	61.4%	61.3%	66.8%
Moderate Maladjustment (Scores 27-33)	35.7%	27.5%	28.2%
Psychiatric Impairment (Scores 34-54)	2.9%	11.2%	5.0 %

Some of the earliest studies seemed to indicate a rather high incidence of maladjustment among teachers. But recent studies show less disturbance among teachers. Nevertheless such teachers do have an effect on their pupils (Barker, 1948 ; Laycock, 1950 ; Symonds, 1954). Crow and Crow (1951) comments that although the number of disturbed teachers is small, there are too many who are suffering from slight maladjustment. To the extent that they themselves are not happy with their work, teachers are certain to fail in their efforts to guide their pupils towards desirable happy life adjustments. Scheier and Cattell (1961) also observe that "some degrees of neurosis exist throughout the population, affecting real life, adjustments and effectiveness. It may be dramatically relevant for only about five per cent of the population, but it has some real relevance to degree of adjustment for the other ninty-five per cent as well."

Necessity of Well-adjusted Teachers in Schools

Judicious re-examination of the earlier data, as pointed out by Kaplan (1959), shows that even in those earlier accounts, teachers differed little from the general public in regard to mental health. Teachers are certainly less likely than non-teachers to be actually committed to some institutions. But this is no great cause for satisfaction, because the teacher in ill health is dissatisfied with almost everything, and he blames the headmaster, other teachers, the climate, or the pupils *etc.*, for things in great part which may be due to his own condition. It must not be forgotten that the ill health may be a result of his fatigue, differences with headmaster, emotional frustration or vocational dissatisfaction, which ultimately affect his teaching, mental health, and learning of even students.

Thus to exemplify, the normal personality reacts to problematic situations and events in a distinctively normal fashion, whereas the neurotic personality reacts in a characteristically symptomatic way to stresses and demands of life. If the neurotic teacher happens to be anxious type, almost every reaction will be coloured by this characteristic and dominating anxiety (Sherman and Jost, 1942). This is why Crow and Crow (1951) say, "Even more important than in industry is the need in the schools for well adjusted, satisfied, and efficient teachers. If we are to be concerned with the mental health of the students, we must assure ourselves, first, that we select as teachers those persons who possess mental health and second, that we do all that is possible to maintain this desirable adjustment."

Indian studies, apart from other foreign studies, which have been abstracted in the following Chapter 2 also indicate the severity of the problem and show the necessity for securing well-adjusted teachers for schools.

Hence the investigator chose the topic :

"Mental Health of Teachers"

CHAPTER 2

Review of Related Studies

A concerted study of the situation of Psycho-diagnosis of maladjustment of pupil-teachers and their Therapy is sufficiently indicated by the studies cited in Chapter 1 before.

An exploration in the field of reported studies of diagnosis of maladjustment of pupil-teachers and their therapy revealed that no special study has been conducted in this area of research except the publication of a few papers (Swainson, 1952 ; Ottaway, 1951), and suggestions (Report of UNESCO Institute for Education, 1955 ; and Recommendation 36, 1953 of XVIth International Conference). Even in the area relating to the personality and adjustment of the teacher and its effects on students, there is hardly any reported research. And research in the area of psycho-therapy is in its formative stage. Only nine doctoral dissertations (Hogan, 1948; Grummon, 1950; Joneitz, 1950 ; Kell, 1950 ; Mosak, 1950 ; Bowman, 1951 ; Fox 1951; Hartley, 1951; and Bown, 1954), four Master's theses have been completed, and at least an equal number were in process (Rogers and Dymond, 1954) in the U.S.A. in 1954. But these researches are not concerned particularly with the psychotherapy of maladjusted teachers and pupil-teachers.

Wall (1955) expressed his surprise about the little research that has gone into elucidating the complexities of the influence on children of the personalities and actions of the teachers. However, there are plenty of sources available for a researcher to pursue in the field of problems of teachers and teacher trainees' characteristics in a wider context of adjustment and effective teaching.

Studies Abroad

Mechane (1940), on the basis of his empirical researches, seemed to have found that emotional adjustment of the teacher is reflected in undesirable emotional reactions of their pupils. Conversely, he indicated that the emotionally stable teachers exercise a beneficial effect upon their pupils.

Symonds (1955) found that superior teachers who are liked by children or pupils in general are found to be personally secure, self-assured and self-integrated.

Yourglich (1955) studied teachers' and students' evaluation of various qualities of an ideal teacher. Factors like understanding, ability to communicate, ability to stimulate, maturity, academic background, responsibility, sense of dedication, sense of humour, cooperativeness, dominance, appearance, friendliness, meticulousness, intelligence, individuality, healthiness, practicability and diligence were considered important.

Cattell and Eber (1957) have isolated five characteristics they considered to be correlated with success in professional occupations : dominance, lack of inhibition, imagination, shrewdness and liberalism, they also noted emotional instability, sobriety, perseverance, sentimentality and self-discipline. From these findings, it appears that there are two types of personalities that are to be found among teachers that are contradictory to each other and provide the basis for success in different aspects of the teacher's role. Thus a teacher with the characteristics of the second type may provide less of a professional image but be more effective teacher.

Johnson-Neyman's technique used by Bowers and Soar (1961) showed that certain relationship achieved statistical significance at extreme positions of deviation ; for example, the best adjusted teachers become more effective following training ; but the less well adjusted teachers become ess effective.

Davies (1961) found only one or two measures among 25 teacher traits to be significantly related to patterns of teaching observed with the ten Flanders' categories. For example, teachers' scores on sub-scale of "warmth" from the Cattell 16 PF Tests and the total Minnesota Teacher Attitude Inventory (MTAI) scores were associated with responsive teacher behaviour as indicated by statistically significant and low positive correlations.

Tarpey (1965) administered a Personality Questionnaire, Intelligence Test, Teacher Attitude Inventory and Interest Inventory to 128 students in four different Training Colleges. She concluded that though the general personality pattern was normal, significant correlation between personality factors and the teaching marks was found in only one college.

In another study of the effects of sensitivity training, Soar (1966) tested the effects of training groups of teachers from four schools, while the principals were given similar training separately. The criterion measures employed were factor scores involving both process and change measurements of pupil products including subject-matter, creativity and personality. No evidence of overall increase in teacher effectiveness as a consequence of the experimental procedure was obtained, but there was an evidence that better adjusted teachers were more effective and less well adjusted teachers were less effective after training than before. These results cross-validated the same finding in the earlier study.

In another study by Arnold (1969) Cattell's 16 PF, Forms A and B, were administered to 78 student teachers. At the close of the student teaching units, the supervising teachers administered the Hoyt-Grim Pupil Reaction Inventory to the students-teachers pupils. This investigation indicated that the 16 PF is a useful objective means for quantifying and profiling personality characteristics of prospective teachers.

Gallop (1970) used 16 PF Test in a study of B. Ed students. The 16 PF analysis indicates that B. Ed. students deviate more from average on factors Q_1 for men and M and G for women, than Certificate students suggesting that B. Ed. men are more radical and free thinking, while B. Ed. women tend to be more imaginative and creative, though less conscientious and persistent, than Certificate women.

Burk (1970) in a paired data study of compatibility took 85 female student-teacher-supervisor teams in elementary education. The sample comprised the qualified seniors of Wisconsin State University-Eau Claire of 1966-67, and their supervisors in the Public Schools of Eau Claire. This study tended to indicate that more successful pairs combined : A. student who scored lower than their supervisors in self-sufficiency, insecurity and independence ; B. Students who were similar to their supervisors in dominance, anxiety, and super-ego ; and in some cases ; C. students who were overwhelmingly more self-sufficient and feminine than their supervisors.

Anderson (1971) took a cross-section study to measure the personality traits as determined by the 16 PF Test. She found that six traits discriminated among male undergraduates and student-teachers and female undergraduates and student-teachers (details not available).

Knapp (1971) attempted to study the teachers' personality, characteristics and rated their effectiveness. He found that the attitudes, needs and personality traits of teachers who are rated as either highly effective or ineffective differ significantly from the attitudes, needs and personality traits of the rating principles.

Indian Studies

A few Indian studies dealing with Personality traits and adjustment of teachers and teacher-trainees are also available.

More than three decades ago Adaval (1952) completed a doctoral level research on the qualities of teachers undertraining. The general qualities which were mentioned are : normal health and or physical fitness, healthy and balanced philosophical and cultural outlook, normal general intelligence, good habits of daily life, a well developed moral life, sociableness and emotional maturity and stability. The specific qualities are : knowledge of the subject concerned, ability to impart knowledge, understanding of and love for children, students leadership and a good command over language.

While studying the relationship between economic status and personality of teachers Saxena (1957) found that education, scholastic standard and economic status were not significantly related to teaching personality.

Another study by Parasher (1961) revealed that pupil-teachers having favourable attitude towards teaching were less neurotic, were self-sufficient, extrovert, dominant, wholesomely, self-conscious and sociable. These pupil-teachers were reported to have some adjustment problems also.

Negi (1962) studied the entrants to the teaching profession and concluded that they were not emotionally, socially and financially well equipped to discharge their duties as teachers in the society.

Some important characteristics of teachers and students were studied by Prasad and Singh (1962). Their finding indicates that the students attach more importance to personality characteristics of a teacher in comparison to their academic characteristics. Students considered characteristics such as honesty, impartiality and good character as more important.

Sarangi (1963) found a positive and substantial (0.44), but not very high positive relationship between emotional maturity and teaching skill.

A study on socio-economic status and its relationship with emotional adjustment and personality of male and female student teachers conducted by Sharma (1963) indicates that male student-teachers in the lower income group and female student-teachers in the higher income group were more emotionally unstable. Similarly, male in the higher income group and female in the lower income group were more introvert.

Bina (1964) studied the relationships between intelligence, social and emotional adjustment and socio-economic factors of female student-teachers and found that these three are positively correlated.

Paul (1968) conducted a comparative study of the personality patterns of engineering, law, medical and teacher-training students taking help of the standardized Rorschach Ink Blot-Test, and found law and teacher-training students emotionally more stable and responsive to social environment than the other two groups.

Raina (1969) administered the California- F-Scale (a measure of anti-democratic potential) to 145 student-teachers. The results indicated that the student-teachers are more authoritarian than some other sample of teacher-educators on whom this instrument has been administered elsewhere (Raina, 1968).

Gupta and Singhal (1971) studied the personality adjustment pattern of 123 male and 121 female pupil-teachers using Saxena's Personality Adjustment Inventory. They have concluded that pupil-teachers are poorly adjusted in comparison to the Saxena's standardization sample.

Prasad (1972) administered 16 PF (Cattell, 1964), but its Hindi Version (Kapoor, 1970) and *Vyaktitva-Parakh-Prashnavali* (Saxena, 1962) to a sample of 52 male and 73 female teacher-trainees to study their personality and adjustment. The following are the findings of his study:

1. In general, both male and female samples are well adjusted in comparison to the general population.
2. Male teacher-trainees are more warm and social (A+), more dominant (E+), more jealous and hard (L+) and more radical (Q_1+) in comparison to their female counterparts.
3. Female teacher-trainees are more intelligent (B+), more sensitive and effeminate (I+), more shrewd, sophisticated and polished (N+), self-sufficient (Q_2+) and having more control and exacting will power (Q_3).
4. Male teacher-trainees are better adjusted in the areas of health, social and emotional adjustment in comparison to the female trainees.
5. There is no sex difference in the areas of Home and College adjustment among the teacher-trainees.
6. Factors C, E, H, O, Q_2 and Q_4 are significantly correlated with the total adjustment as well as one or more adjustment areas. These factors show significant relationships on t-test and correlational studies.
7. Poorly adjusted group of teacher-trainees is definitely scoring higher on second order anxiety component factors.
8. Poorly adjusted group also shows higher neurotic trends as their scores on second order Neuroticism component factors are higher.

Ahuja (1975) studied mental health of 50 student-teachers (27 males and 23 females). He found that 90 per cent of the sample has average mental health. Only 2 per cent belong to the category of border line mental inefficiency which is due to the pressure of circumstances. The percentage of subjects whose NQ is 55 and who can be termed 'neurotic' is 8. Out of these 6 per cent come under the category of 'highly neurotic.' Female student-teachers score higher than male teachers. The mean difference in favour of female student-teachers is significant at 5 per cent level.

CHAPTER 3

Conceptual Framework of the Study

A. Need and Importance of the Study

This brief review of related studies indicates the dearth of attempts made to study the problem of adjustment of teachers and teacher-trainees. Emphasis has been laid towards the problem of psycho-diagnosis of maladjustment of pupil-teacher and their therapy. Hence the need to study the problem of adjustment of teachers has been emphasised in the following words as reported in the Second Survey of Research in Education (Ed. Buch 1979).

> ...While the interest in this area of study (Adjustment problems) still seems to persist in the researchers, these studies do not go beyond surveying or comparing the adjustment patterns of selected groups of students. Secondly, concentration is mostly on students like in other personality studies, and the teachers seem to have been badly neglected—may be sometimes it is taken for granted that the teachers are well adjusted. This is something that needs to be explored at this stage, of the research on personality adjustment. Here again environmental cor-

relates of adjustment both in the teachers and students, job satisfaction or work motivation of students, the possibilities enhancing the school adjustment of students by environmental variation or by teachers' behaviour modification *etc.* need to be studied. Perhaps before that, the dynamics of school adjustment also needs to be further explored.

The development of an adequate personality in all those who will teach children is the first aim of teacher-training. Hence during the teacher-training programme itself the emphasis should be on psycho-diagnosis of maladjustment of teacher-trainees and maladjusted trainees should be helped or diagnosed through counselling for their better adjustment. Crow and Crow (1951) also observe that :

> ...No amount of pre-teacher training can assure a prospective teacher that he will be able to exert hygienic influence as a teacher in a classroom. It is not until his personality and those of his individuals pupils have a possibility of interaction that he can predict what his influence will be. He may be healthy and well groomed, use excellent English, and speak clearly and correctly, all characteristics that are essential to and predisposed toward successful teaching, but the test of excellence lies in his own emotional stability, his understanding of pupil personality, and all those other traits that are inherent in the adjustment pattern of a teacher.

A good number of young teachers go to schools with neuroses untouched during the training course, neuroses which frequently lead to breakdown during the first few years of teaching, or to severe personality problems in later life with consequent unfortunate repercussions on the children or pupils concerned. At the student stage a great many problems which cause severe anxiety are relatively slight in nature and yield to a few sessions with a trained psychological adviser or counsellor. This responsibility which the psychological specialist can well undertake by passing on those cases which require more prolonged treatment, he can send than to available psychological or psychiatric services outside (UNESCO Institute for Education, 1955). Recommendation 36 (1953) of Geneva Conference also suggests that :

> ...It is desirable that all candidates should undergo psychological examination immediately before and during training, with a view to eliminating those possessing anomalies of character of behaviour which are incompatible with teaching ; entrance examinations can be with advantage supplemented by interviews and, if necessary, by short periods of probation.

"In a hygiene programme", say Pressey, Robinson and Horrocks (1967), "the teacher-in-training develops skills for handling frustrating situations. Actually not much is known about the possibilities here, effective skills are needed, rather than 'tricks.' There is need for research on the methods particularly effective people use in handling frustrating situations."

Principals and senior lecturers of colleges of Education are often heard complaining that some pupil-teachers do show erratic and aberrant behaviour which may be labelled as maladjusted. The reasons for this are many, for example, it is so because trainees are not selected with the help of any personality screening test, or trainees usually come from such socio-economic stratum of the society which cannot remain unaffected by such malady, or the activities and experiences of the training college itself are so very stressful and likely to create tension that they create maladjustment in the pupil-teacher *etc., etc.* Whatever the reason, one has to accept the observations as qualified and at its face value. It should be the concern of educationists that such maladjustment should be detected at proper time and nipped in the bud. Ahrens (1952) has also emphasised that "it is imperative that we get at the source of tensions and find ways of eliminating or reducing them." This investigator, therefore, realized the need of psycho-diagnosis of maladjustment in the pupil-teachers community and to eradicate that problem in the larger interest of education. As such he planned to pursue experimental study in this area which does not seem to have been attempted in our country seriously.

Purposes of the Study

The general aim of the study was to gain objective knowledge in regard to the end results and process of one form of psychotherapy-non-directive approach. Without trying to use such unsatisfactory global concepts as 'success' or 'failure', it was desired to learn more precisely what the measurable concomitants of a period non-directive therapy are. However, the following purposes of the present study has been delineated :

1. To identify maladjusted pupil-teachers.
2. To find out sex-wise proportion of maladjusted pupil-teachers.
3. To give them therapy for their better adjustment.
4. To observe the change occurred in maladujusted pupil-teachers during wait, therapy and follow-up periods.
5. To popularise the utility of methodology employed in the study if it is successful.

Hypotheses

Keeping in view of the above objectives the following hypotheses were constructed for this study :

1. Subjects motivated for therapy will improve over a period of no therapy (wait-period).
2. There will be improvement in experimental group during therapy.
3. There will be larger improvement in females than males of experimental group during therapy.
4. Therapy (Experimental) group will show improvement in the follow-up.

Delimitations

1. The study was restricted to maladjusted pupil-teachers so diagnosed from amongst the teacher-trainees studying for B. Ed. degree during the session 1981-82 in

Janata College of Education, Chandrapur (Maharashtra).

2. Neuroticism Scale Questionnaire—The NSQ (Scheier and Cattell, 1961, its Hindi Version by Kapoor and Kapoor, 1974) was used to diagnose maladjustment and adjustment in pupil-teachers.
3. Non-directive therapy (Rogers, 1942) was employed for treating maladjusted pupil-teachers.
4. Percentage, t-test and case study were used in analysing the data.

Basic Assumptions and Definitions

In this part operational definitions of some of the repeated terms used in this report are given :

(i) Psychodiagnosis

Psychodiagnosis is the identification of the psychological characteristics of an individual with the aid of special methods. There are two types of procedures in psycho-diagnosis. One may be described as statistical or psychometric, the other clinical or intuitive (Eysenck *et. al.*, 1972).

In the clinical or intuitive method the psychologist combines the results that have been obtained, his observations and his information based on psychological insight and knowledge and on his personal experience ; whereas in the statistical method correct interpretation depends on the reliability and integrity of the definition of dependence, and stands or falls, as in the clinical method, on the psychological insight and experience of the psychologist. Meehl (1954) established both methods lead to approximately the same number of correct results. However, a comparison would, therefore, necessarily favour the statistical method.

In the present study statistical (psychometric) method was used to identify maladjustment in pupil-teachers with the help of Neuroticism Scale Questionnaire—the NSQ (Hindi Version by Kapoor and Kapoor, 1961). Because NSQ scores discriminate not only between neurotics and normals, but also between varying degrees of slighter neurotic trend in persons usually classed as normal. Thus the NSQ can be usefully applied to the vast numbers of essentially normal persons for whom assessment of neurotic trend is nevertheless important in occupational acceptability and in understanding and improving adjustment and proficiency (Scheier and Cattell, 1961).

(*ii*) *Maladjustment*

Life is a continuous process of adjustment, in which we strive to meet our own needs and maintain harmonious relations with our environment. When an individual deals with his problems effectively he is said to be well-adjusted—to be adapting successfully to both the inner and outer demands being made upon him. Conversely, when his problems prove too much for him—as shown by anxiety, inefficiency, unhappiness, or a more serious symptoms—he is referred to as maladjusted (Coleman, (1964). Thus maladjustment is an inability to adjustment to one's own, social, vocational, or environmental demands.

Maladjustment may be conceived as (a) a disequilibrium brought about by the interaction of the individual and on environment which denies satisfaction to any of the primary needs ; and as (b) a state generally of slow growth and representing an accumulation of experiences rather than a dramatic clash with the environment or 'trauma' (Wall, 1955).

If an individual's adjustments are so inadequate that they cause him chronic discomfort, and interfere markedly with his efficiency in ordinary living, they may be characterized as psychoneurotic or neurotic... The psychoneuroses are not specific entities or diseases, but represent certain range of severity in the continuum of maladjustments (Boring, Langfeld and Weld ; 1951).

In the present study maladjustment means higher scores than average on each of the four neuroticism components of the NSQ and/or the total composite neuroticism level obtained by the pupil-teachers.

Thus maladjustment is a symptom which calls for investigation and for preventive and curative actions as early as possible,

(iii) Pupil-teachers

The term pupil-teacher refer to one who is acquiring practical teaching experience and skill under the guidance of a critic teacher or other supervisor in the special laboratory or practice school of a teacher training institution or in the classes of a public or private school ; usually an advanced student who has had no other teaching experience (Good, 1945).

In the present study graduates and postgraduates undergoing B. Ed. training programme of Janata College of Education, Chandrapur (Maharashtra) have been designated as pupil-teachers.

(iv) Psychotherapy

It means literally treatment of the mind, refers to any variety of psychological means used to modify mental, emotional and behavioural disorders. This may involve individual interviews where therapist and patient verbally explore the the patient's conflicts, feelings, memories and fantasies in order to attain insight into the causes of the present problems, or it may be conducted in small groups of six to twelve patients, or, in the case of children may take the form of play between child and therapist during which the child expresses feelings and learns new behaviour through the relationship with the therapist (Eysenck, 1975).

Shaffer (1951) in Boring, Langfeld and Weld (1951) have said that psychological treatment is usually called counselling or psychotherapy. The aim of counselling or psychotherapy is to release the individual from inhibitions and repressions and to give him improved insight into his own conflicts and adjustments, so that he can work out a more satisfactory solution to his problems.

There are varieties of psychotherapies which are employed, in treating maladjusted people. But in the present context Non-Directive Therapy of Rogers (1942) was used in helping the maladjusted pupil-teachers in their proper adjustment.

(V) *Non-Directive Therapy*

The wound of a badly injured arm must heal itself, and the surgeon who treats such a wound merely arranges matters so that self-healing proceeds under optimal conditions. There is possibly more than a mere analogy between this bodily regeneration and the way in which non-directive counselling avails itself of the curative forces within cach unique personality (Carmichael, 1947).

The major factor which differentiates the non-directive method from others is that it is client-centred. It means that the direction of the therapy process is essentially in the hands of the client rather than in those of the counsellor. The individual, and not his symptoms, is the focus of the therapy. This method of therapy, in contrast with some others, is directed towards the achievement of the integration and independence of the client in the minimum necessary time.

Rogers (1944) holds that there are two basic assumptions essential to the non-directive method. The first assumption is that the counsellor recognizes the personal integrity and self-directedness of the individual. The second tenet is that the individual has an enormous capacity for adaptation. This means that, if the individual is placed in a favourable counselling situation, he possesses within himself the drive to achieve a more satisfactory level of adjustment. It is also a part of this assumption that, if the individual is in a situation in which he is unhampered by his usual emotional barriers, he will find the means by which this level of adjustment can be attained. As a result of this assumption, there is in non-directive therapy, as compared with directive treatment, much less emphasis on the process of diagnosis and more emphasis on the methods of freeing the client from the emotional blocks which prevent his favourable growth.

Thus real non-directive counsslling depends on nurturing a wholesome growth from within the individual personality of the client who is being counselled.

In the present context basic principles of non-directive therapy (Rogers, 1944) were followed in the process of giving non-directive counselling the maladjusted pupil-teachers.

CHAPTER 4

Procedure

DESCRIPTION OF TEST

A. Description of Neuroticism Scale Questionnaire (The NSQ) Used

The Neuroticism Scale Questionnaire is designed to in such a way so that it can evaluate the extent of neurotic problems in a person or group of persons before active action can be taken.

It is simple, brief (40 items, 5 to 10 minutes), easy to administer to individuals or groups and above all it makes it easy to score by standard key-scoring system. It helps diagnosis by giving a quantitative evaluation of neurotic trend without consuming the time of skilled practioners, leaving them free to concentrate on guidance, therapy, *etc.*

NSQ scores discriminate not only between neurotic and normals, but also between varying degrees of slighter neurotic trend present in persons generally classified as normal. Thus, the NSQ can be usefully applied to the vast number of essentially normal persons for whom assessment of neurotic trend is nevertheless important in occupational acceptability and in understanding and improving adjustment and proficiency.

The NSQ is rooted firmly, by validation research, in the common core of clinical judgement regarding the symptoms and nature of neurosis (Scheier and Cattell, 1961).

Hindi verson of the NSQ (Kapoor and Kapoor, 1966, 1974) is also available along with the Norm Table for converting NSQ Raw Score to Stens (Ten points standard scores).

Each item of the NSQ has three response al'ernatives, scored, 0, 1, 2, from lower to higher level of neuroticism and any single item contributes to only one of the four components. The total composite neuroticism score is simply the sum of raw scores on all 40 items in the four components. This amounts to an approximately equal weighting of each component in its contribution to total neuroticism. This weighting is essentially proportional to the relative sharpness with which these components discriminate between neurotics and normals, except that the anxiety component is slightly under-weighted.

A left-side response contributes to high score as often as a right side response, and, in each component except anxiety, a "yes" or "agree" response contributes to high score as often as a "no" or "disagree" response. In the anxiety-component, high score is more often associated "yes" than with "no" because tendency to agree, in any type of item, is known to associate with higher anxiety level (Cattell and Scheier, 1958 and 1961). The "yes-ness" in keying anxiety items thus adds to their intrinsic effectiveness as anxiety-measuring items.

The test is arranged in a four page booklet. The front cover page gives instructions for taking the test, and the other three pages serve both as examples as well as buffers. The test proper follows on the inside two pages, 20 items to a page in cyclical order as between the four components, and with the least threatening items placed earlier in the rest, wherever possible. The back cover page contains arrangements for recording of test scores as well as for related clinical comment.

Thus, the NSQ provides basic measures for each factored personality dimension. This test is designed to give a properly weighted total on some six personality dimensions. Unlike the 16 PF Test (Cattell and Stice, 1957), it does not set out to measure the entire personality, but deals only with that portion of it most intimately bound up with and expressing neurotic trend.

(i) Description of the Neurotic-Associated Personality Factors Measured by the NSQ

The six neurosis-associated dimensions of personality are described in Table 4.1. The fuller discussion and interpretation of each of these factors are given in the Handbook of the NSQ (Scheier and Cattell, 1961) and elsewhere (Cattell, 1957; Cattel and Scheir, 1961 ; Cattell and Stice, 1957).

TABLE 4.1

Description of Neuroticism Scale Questionnaire (NSQ)

Low Score Description	Alphabetical Designation of Factors	High Score Description
TOUGH Tough Mindedness	I	SENSITIVE Over-protection, Tender-minded, Cultured, Protected, Emotional, Sensitivity
CHEERFUL Happy-go-lucky Cheerfulness	F	DEPRESSIVE Depressiveness, Inhibited, sober, seriousness
DOMINANT Dominance	E	SUBMISSIVE Submissiveness, Suggestibility, Dependence
ASSURED Assured self-Confidence	O	WORRIED Worried, Guilt Proneness
CALM Calm Relaxation	Q4	TENSE Ergic Tension (from frustration)
EMOTIONALLY MATURED Ego Strength	C	EMOTIONALLY IMMATURED Ego Weakness or Emotional Immaturity & Instability
NOT-ANXIETY ↙		↘ ANXIETY

(*ii*) *Reliability and Validity of the NSQ*

Reliabilities

The consistency coefficients (split-half, corrected to full length), obtained on the sample of 300 normal cases : 200 males and 100 females (average age 31 years) are reported in Table 4.2 (Scheier and Cattell, 1961).

TABLE 4.2

Reliability Coefficients for the Neuroticism Scale Questionnaire (NSQ). Split-Half Consistency Coefficients

Tender Mindedness	Depression	Submissiveness	Anxiety	Total Test Neuroticism Score
I	F	E		
+.55	+.57	+.47	+.70	+.67

Validities

Two types of validities are reported : Concept (construct) and concrete (Cattell, 1957).

(a) Concept or construct validity is the correlation of the items in a given scale with factor (concept, dimension, functional unity) they are designed to measure. The concept validities for each of the four NSQ components are as follows :

Tender-Mindedness (I) = +.74 ; Depression (F) = +.76 ;

Submissiveness (E) = +. 69 ; Anxiety = +.84

From the split-half reliability of each component (Table 4.2), assuming that the items have no specifics in common, but only a common factor, where

$$\text{validity} = \sqrt{\text{reliability}}$$

(b) Concrete validity is the correlation of the test with the life performances and categories, in short, with a "pointed out" criterion in every day life.

The NSQ was administered to 1(2 clinically-judged neurotics (53 males and 49 females) at ten different institutional centres. The 102 neurotics' total NSQ scores were found to be considerably higher than those for 1,068 normals, the difference being confirmed at a very high level of statistical confidence (beyond the .0005 level ; (Scheier and Cattell, 1961). That is, the NSQ is very definitely a test of neurosis in the concrete validity clinical criterion sense, for neurotics scores significantly higher than normals on it.

(iii) Test Administration

The test is administered without a time limit, but typically requires no more than five to ten minutes for clients who are not severely disturbed and are above seventh or eighth grade of educational level.

The test can be administered to one individual a time or in group form to as many as several hundred persons at one time.

The test instructions and items are clear and easy enough so that self-administration is feasible for clients who possess a minimum of responsibility. In such cases, examinees should be reminded that they are to complete every item on the test, and that they should not consult with anyone else in deciding their answers.

The NSQ can be readministered to the same persons at intervals of as little as two weeks, *e.g.*, to determine fluctuations in neuroticism level over time and/or in response to therapy or other conditions, for subjects apparently show negligible memory for particular responses made, after two weeks or more.

(iv) Scoring of the NSQ

The complete test booklet is the usual record for obtaining the score. The test is scored directly from the test booklet. This is scored by a streamlined stencil key.

Before scoring the test, the test booklet is scanned to ascertain that one and only one answer has been marked for each question. When this condition is not met, the test booklet is returned to the examinee to complete it properly. If this is not possible, items not marked in any way by the examinee should be given as score. Where more than one answer is marked for an item, the investigator should proceed as follows :

Marked	Score as if
Middle category and one extreme	Only the extreme marked
Both extreme categories or all three categories	Middle category marked

Reading off the raw scores and adding to give the total neuroticism scores, the scoring stencil is placed on the test booklet. Simple, standard rules for placing and using the key are printed on the key itself (Scheier and Cattell, 1961 and The Psycho-Centre, 1966, 1974).

Raw scores obtained can be converted to standard normative scores, if desired.

(*v*) *Norms*

The norm used for this study is not the American norm provided by Scheier and Cattell (1961), but the Indian norm prepared by Kapoor and Kapoor (1966, 1974) on their Hindi Version of the NSQ.

B. Description of Non-Directive Therapy

Non-directive approach of psychotherapy or counselling is formulated by Carl R. Rogers (1942, 1951, 1959, 1961). A basic assumption of this thereapy is that the patient has the right to solve his own problems and select his own life goals.

The aim of this therapy is to assist the patient and attain responsible maturity so that he can more effectively cope with present and future difficulties.

Chaplin (1968) describes the basic conditions of the therapeutic process of Rogers (1951). For therapy to occur, it is necessary that these conditions exist :

1. Two persons are in contact.
2. That the first person, whom we shall term the client, is is in a state of incongruence, being vulnerable, or anxious.

3. That the second person, who we shall term the therapist, is congruent in relationship.
4. That the therapist is experiencing unconditional positive regard towards the client.
5. That the therapist is experiencing an empathic understanding of the client's internal frame of reference.
6. That the client perceives, at least to a minimal degree, conditions 4 & 5, the unconditional positive regard of therapist for him, and the empathic understanding of the therapist.

Rogers (1942) has considered the therapeutic process itself to be orderly and predictable, typically by following the five steps.

1. *The Client comes for help.* During the first interview with the patient the therapeutic situation is defined. The counsellor makes it clear that he does not have all the answers but the therapy situation will provide a place where the patient can work out his own solutions.

2. *Expression of feeling.* By his permissive and accepting attitude, the therapist encourages the free expression of feelings and now negative emotions that have been bottled up inside the patients are permitted to get released for the first time.

As these negative feelings come spilling into the open it is therapist's function to recognize, accept and clarify them and assumptions underlying the patient's problems. This is done in such a way that the client can recognize his feelings and assumptions and make way for free expression so that nothing is hidden that troubles him.

When the patient's negative feelings have fully expressed, they are followed by faint and tentative expressions of positive feelings.

These positive feelings likewise are recognized, clarified and accepted without praise or blame in such a way that the patient can accept them, as part of himself without the need to feel defensive about them.

3. *Development of Insight* : Gradually this increased recognition and acceptance of the real self leads to the development of insight or understanding. Among the most

important elements of insight emphasised by Rogers are (a) the experiencing, understanding, and acceptance of aspects which he/she has previously repressed, (b) a clearer understanding of the causes behind his/her behaviour and improved integration, and (c) a clarification of possible courses of positive action.

4. *Positive Steps* : Although the first positive steps worked out by the client may not be dramatic, they are stepping stones in the right direction and with time, as these minor positive actions bring satisfaction and increased feelings of adequacy and self-assurance, the client moves toward positive growth and development.

5. *Ending the Contacts* : As the client graduates from fearful and tentatively undertaken positive actions to an increasingly confident integration of positive and self-directed actions, there is a feeling of decreasing need for help and a recognition on the part of the client that the therapeutic relationship must end. The decision to terminate, like the earlier decisions to attempt positive actions, comes from the client. By terminating the contacts under his own initiative, he has taken the final step towards independence. For he has now assumed a full measure of responsibility for his own life.

In order to make more understandable the type of statements of both client and counsellor in non-directive counselling situation, a system of categories was devised by which the various statements might be classified. Snyder (1945 and 1947) describes the counsellor categories, client content categories and client feeling categories.

The following are the counsellor categories :

1. Structuring-statements which explain the counselling procedure ; responses which state the expected outcome of the treatment, or the limitations of time, or the responsibilities of the counsellor or client.

   Example : "I am not interested in the least in either asking, suggesting or telling you to do something that you really fundamentally may not want to do. I am interested however, in talking and thinking these things through with you so that you feel what you are doing is really what you want to do."

2. Direct Question—Questions in which the counsellor asks for information ; a directive technique.

   Examples : "When did you first start having these feelings ?" "This seems to be a battle that you must carry out yourself, it is that it ?"

3. Forcing Client Responsibility—Attempts by the counsellor to redirect to the client the responsibility for selecting the topic to be discussed ; a directive technique.

   Examples : "Well, how do you feel about that ?" "You feel that's the problem ?"

4. Non-directive Leads—Responses of the counsellor which elicit further statement by the client of his problem. These responses are planned in such a manner as to avoid limiting the nature of the discussion to any narrow topic.

   Examples : "What's on your mind today ?" "How are things going ?" "Do you want to tell me more about that ?"

5. Acceptance—Simple agreement ; statements that indicate understanding or assent, but do not imply approval or disapproval.

   Examples : "Yes." "I see". "No" (following a negative statement).

6. Restatement of Content—Repetitions of the idea expressed by the client which do not recognize the statement in such a manner as to reveal more clearly the client's feelings ; those statements which reflect more of the intellectual aspect of what the client has said than of the feeling tone. A counsellor response can be classified as restatement of content only when the classifier is aware of the client statement which has preceded it.

7. Clarification of Feeling—Reponses by the counsellor which reorganize or synthesize the feelings expressed by the client. The mere changing of the client's wording does not necessarily constitute clarification of feeling. As with restatement of content, counsellor responses can be classified as clarification of feeling only when the classifier is aware of the client statement which has preceded it.

8. Interpretation—Counsellor responses which indicate casual relationships, or which respond to feelings that have not been expressed by the client. These statements frequently represent the counsellor's interjection of his "diagnostic" concepts into the interview, and they are semi-directive in character. Interpretation; like restatement of content and clarification of feeling, can be classified as such only when the classifier is aware of the client statement which preceded the counsellor response. What may be in one situation a clarification of feeling, may in another context represent interpretation or restatement of content.

9. Approval—Counsellor statement which evaluate the client or his ideas in terms of the counsellor's own attitudes in a such manner as to provide emotional support ; a semi-directive technique.

   Examples : "That's right." "That's a very interesting comment and may well be worth considering again." "I believe that is good rule of personality."

10. Reassurance—Counsellor statements which encourage the client, which are intended to raise the client's self-esteem or self-assurance, or which imply sympathy ; a semi-directive technique.

    Examples : "I can see how you feel." "You know that I will be glad to help if I can." "And it's really not unusual ; that sort of thing happens a good bit."

11. Information—Statements supplying factual data or the expression of an opinion ; a directive counselling technique.

12. Miscellaneous—Statements which are not described by the other categories. This includes friendly conversation, ending of the contact or of the series of interviews etc.

Client-content categories are described below :

1. Problem—statements indicating areas of concern to the client, or revealing symptoms of maladjustment or dissatisfaction, or statements which report situations or incidents relating to the client's problem.
2. Asking for information—any question of the client which request a factual reply from the counsellor. These frequently include requests for advice or for reassurance.
3. Disagreement—rejection of, or reluctance to accept, any statement of the counsellor.

   Examples : "That's not always true," "Well, it's exactly that."
4. Answering Questions—a reply to a direct question. Simple acceptance of a counsellor's clarification of feeling is not included.

   Examples of answers : "Yes, I would like to go ahead with counselling." "No, no, I don't."
5. Agreement—simple acceptance of a counsellor's clarification of feeling. "Yes". "That's exactly it."
6. Insight—statements by the client indicating a recognition of the causes of his behaviour or revealing a reorganization in his understanding of himself. This does not include rationalizations.
7. Planning—statements revealing the client's decisions regarding future actions or intentions to change his attitudes. Discussions of previous plans are excluded.
8. Miscellaneous—statements which are not described by the other categories. This includes friendly conversation, ending of the contact or of the series of interviews, *etc*.

Client-feeling categories are as follows :

1. Positive Attitude—statements which reveal approval and acceptance of the client himself, the counsellor or the counselling process, or other persons, objects, or situation."

   Examples : "I am really greatly improved." "Every time I come here, when I go home I feel more relaxed, more at peace with people. I guess it's just because I have had this chance of letting off steam."

2. Negative Attitudes—statements which reveal disapproval or rejection of the client himself, the counsellor, or the counselling process, or other persons, objects or situations.

   Examples : "This is all perfectly silly, but the doctor insisted that I come in and see you" "I always felt that other fellows could always to things, but I could never come up to the other group."

3. Ambivalent Attitudes—statements which reveal the concurrent existence of favourable and unfavourable attitudes toward the client himself, the counsellor, or the counselling process, or other persons, objects, or situations.

   Examples : "I want to find out but I am afraid to."

C. Preliminary Try-out

There is just one institution of secondary teacher-training in this district where this research was proposed to be conducted. Hence Neuroticism Scale Questionnaire—The NSQ (Scheier and Cattell, 1961)—but its Revised Hindi Version (Ka; oor and Kapoor 1974) Appendix I was administered to all the 14 teacher-educators of the College of Education for preliminary try-out of the study to see if there was any ambiguity, difficulty to answer any item and any other disturbing factor in the administration of the test. The colleagues were not familiar with the test (The NSQ).

They were informed, apart from other necessary instructions, that the test generally takes 10 to 12 minutes to be completed. They volunteered to take the test. Upon administration, they answered all the items of the test within its expected time without any difficulty. None of them reported any difficulty, or ambiguity in the language of the test, or difficulty in understanding concepts involved in the items or feeling of fatigue or discomfort.

The preliminary try-out using this tool was done with yet another purpose in mind. It was to ascertain the sensitivity of the tool as to whether it can discriminate between normal and neurotic and also whether it can reflect the various degrees of maladjustment of the individuals on whom it is administered.

In this try-out of 14 colleagues the following picture emerged :

Table 4.3 shows that 42.86 per cent (6 teacher-educators) of the 14 teacher-educators were maladjusted.

TABLE 4.3

Percentage of Maladjusted Teacher-Educators

Number of Teacher-Educators participated in test admn.	Number of Maladjusted Teacher-educators identified	Percentage of Maladjusted Teacher-Educatiors
14	6	42.86

Table 4.4 describes their various degrees of maladjustment.

TABLE 4.4

Degree-wise break-up of Maladjusted Teacher-Educators

Total Raw Score obtained	49-53	52-53	56	58	Total
Total sten score	7	8	9	10	
Number of Teacher-Educators who obtained these scores	2	2	1	1	6

Table 4.4 shows that two maladjusted teacher-educators scored 49 to 50 and they reached sten 7, another two obtained the scores 52 and 53, hence their sten scores were 8, and one teacher-educator's score was 56 and other one's 58, so their stens were 9 and 10 respectively. However, all six of them were above average in the sten range, but they had varying degrees of maladjustment.

Thus it is clear from the above tables that the tool is sensitive enough and proper for use in this study.

After preliminary try-out of the test on a small sample of teacher-educators, the investigator proceeded to administer this test to all the 110 teacher-trainees of the College to identify maladjustment, if any, in them. And after the first administration of the test, its administration was repeated to only maladjusted pupil-teachers (who were kept in experimental and control (groups at three different tests points (pre, post and follow-up) to know their improvement of therapy.

D. Subjects and Over-all Design of the Study

(i) Subjects

The subjects were selected from 110 pupil-teachers undergoing B. Ed. training programme of Janata College of Education, Chandrapur, Maharashtra (India). Through the administration of a diagnostic test—the NSQ (Scheier and Cattell, 1961), the Hindi Version (Kapoor and Kapoor, 1974) of this Test (Appendix-I) 40 pupil-teachers obtained above average scores on the NSQ. Hence, they were diagnosed as maladjusted, and considered as subjects for the present study, Table 4.5 shows the complete picture of pupil-teachers who scored above average on the NSQ.

However, these subjects were divided stratifically and proportionately into two groups—experimental (therapy) and control (no-therapy) for the study. The subjects represented a variety of degrees of maladjustments on the NSQ's different scores. Table 4.6 shows the selection of therapy (experimental) group.

Thus, in therapy or experimental group, there were 23 maladjusted subjects, among them 15 were males and 8 were

TABLE 4.5
Pupil-Teachers who Scored High on the NSQ

Pupil-Teacher	Sex	Age	Total NSQ Raw score	score Sten Score
I.R.	M	27	55	9
S.B.	F	21	51	7
A.M.	M	23	51	7
G.B.	M	30	51	7
V.G.	M	24	49	7
V.T.	M	30	53	8
D.R.	M	25	50	7
M.S.	M	30	51	7
U.C.	M	37	55	9
S.B.C.	F	25	56	9
V.V.	M	32	51	7
Y.T.	M	21	49	7
D.D.	M	28	54	8
K.J.	F	27	50	7
R.H.	M	24	53	8
G.V.	M	26	50	7
M.M.	M	27	56	9
H.H.	M	26	49	7
S.P.K.	M	23	49	7
M.K.	M	25	50	7
R.N.	M	30	54	8
V.L.	M	40	54	8
K.C.	M	41	52	8
R.M.	M	23	52	8
A.L.	M	26	51	7
S.P.	F	26	53	8
M.N.	F	23	57	10
R.S.P.	M	25	49	7
B.M.	M	23	54	8
S.R.	F	22	60	10
M.N.R.	M	27	49	7
S.S.	F	21	56	9
K.N.	F	21	50	7
R.S.	F	25	56	9
D.K.	M	38	51	7
N.V.	F	24	61	10
S B.W.	M	30	50	7
T.D.	M	28	51	7
S.H.	F	24	51	7
S.K.	M	27	51	7

TABLE 4.6

Selection of Therapy (Experimental Group) from all Maladjusted Cases on the Basis of Their Scores Obtained on the NSQ

Total Raw Score		49-51	52-54	55-56	57-61	Total No. of subjects	Per cent
Total Sten Score		7	8	9	10		
Number of subjects who obtained these scores sex-wise and their proportion in 50%							
	M	17	8	3	0	28	100
		8.5 9	4	1.5 2		15	50
	F	5	1	3	3	12	100
		2.5 3	.5 1	1.5 2	1.5 2	8	50
	T	22	9	5	3	40	100
		12	5	4	2	23	50

M=Male ; F = Female ; T = Total

famales. The rest of 17 maladjusted subjects were kept in no-therapy (control group). Table 4.7 shows the composition of both the groups.

TABLE 4.7
Composition of Therapy (Experimental and no-Therapy (Control) Groups

Sten & Raw Scores Group		7 49-51	8 52-54	9 55-56	10 57-51
Number of cases in Therapy or Experimental Group					
(M—15)	M	9	4	2	0
(F=8)	F	3	1	2	2
(T=23)	T	12	5	4	2
Number of cases in No-therapy or Control Group					
(M=13)	M	8	4	1	0
(F=4)	F	2	0	1	1
(T=17)	T	10	4	2	1

The choice of the subjects was made to make an intensive study of a group of moderate size rather than a superficial analysis of a larger number.

(a) Therapy of Experimental Group

The therapy group consists of twenty-three subjects in the age group of between 21 and 40 years with an average 26 years. There were 15 men and 8 women ; all were the pupil-teachers. Table 4.8 gives the clear picture of therapy group.

(b) No-therapy (Control) Group

The no-therapy (control) group consists of those subjects who were not seeking counselling (therapy) but who were paid to take test at intervals corresponding to those of continuers (experimental group).

There were 17 subjects in the no-therapy (control) group ranging in the age between 21 and 41 years, with an average 27 years. There were 13 men and 4 women ; all were the pupil-teachers. Table 4.9 clarifies the status of the subjects of no-therapy (control) group.

TABLE 4.8
Subjects in the Therapy Group
N=23

Case No.	Subjects	Sex	Age
1.	I.R.	M	27
2.	S.B.	F	21
3.	A.M.	M	23
4.	G.B.	M	30
5.	V.G.	M	24
6.	M.S.	F	30
7.	Y.T.	M	21
8.	V.V.	M	32
9.	D.D.	M	28
10.	K.J.	F	27
11.	R.H.	M	24
12.	M.M.	M	27
13.	H.H.	M	26
14.	M.K.	M	25
15.	R.N.	M	30
16.	V.L.	M	40
17.	A.L.	M	26
18.	S.P.	F	26
19.	M.N.	F	23
20.	S.R.	F	22
21.	S.S.	F	21
22.	R.S.	F	25
23.	S.K.	M	27

TABLE 4.9

Subjects in No-Therapy (Control) Group

Sr. No. of Cases	Subjects	Sex	Age
1.	V.T.	M	30
2.	D.R.	M	25
3.	U.C.	M	37
4.	S.B.C.	F	25
5.	G.V.	M	26
6.	S.P.K.	M	23
7.	K.C.	M	41
8.	R.M.	M	23
9.	R.S.P,	M	25
10.	B.M.	M	23
11.	M.N.R.	M	27
12.	K.N.	F	21
13.	D.K.	M	38
14.	N.V.	F	24
15.	S.B.W.	M	30
16.	T,D.	M	28
17.	S.H.	F	24

(c) Composition of Therapy (Experimental and No-Therapy (Control) Groups

These two groups were also matched for age, sex, academic status and in general for their problem Table 4.10 gives the composition of both the groups.

TABLE 4.10

Total Group Characteristics for All Therapy (Experimental) and No-Therapy (Control) Subjects

Group	Age		Sex		Academic Status	Problem
	Range	Mean	M	F		
Therapy (Experimental) Group N=23	21-40	26.30	15	8	Pupil-Teacher	Maladjusted
No-Therapy (Control) Group N=17	21-41	27.65	13	4	Pupil-Teacher	Maladjusted

It is clear from the Table 4.10 that matching is satisfactory on academic status, nature of the problem and to some extent on age factor, though moderately satisfactory on one variable, *i.e.* sex.

(d) Attrition Group

Those subjects who failed to take and/or discontinue counselling and failed to complete five or more therapeutic interview were called the members of attrition group. Thus the therapy (experimental) group was also sub-divided into the attrition group and the continuers group on the basis of number of therapeutic interviews received and taking part in different test points once therapy was begun. The nine subjects who continued their therapy for three or less interviews and/or took part in one or two test-points were labelled the attrition group. Subjects of attrition group are shown in Table 4.11.

TABLE 4.11

Subjects of Attrition Group

S. No. of Cases from the Experimental Group	Subjects	Sex	Age
2	S.B.	F	21
3	A.M.	M	23
4	G.B.	M	30
6	M.S.	F	30
8	V.V.	M	32
9	D.D.	M	28
16	V.L.	M	40
21	S.S.	F	21
23	S.K.	M	27

(e) Continuers Group

The continuers group consists of 14 subjects (9 males and 5 females) who remained in therapy for at least five therapeutic interviews and completed all test points. Most of these subjects stayed in treatment much longer.

(ii) Method of Data Collection

The Neuroticism Scale Questionnaire—the NSQ (Scheier and Cattell, 1961), the Hindi Version (Kapoor and Kapoor, 1974) of the test was used to measure adjustment and maladjustment of a group of subjects before therapy, after completion of a therapy and a follow-up point six months to one year later.

The Figure 4.1 describes the points of test administration.

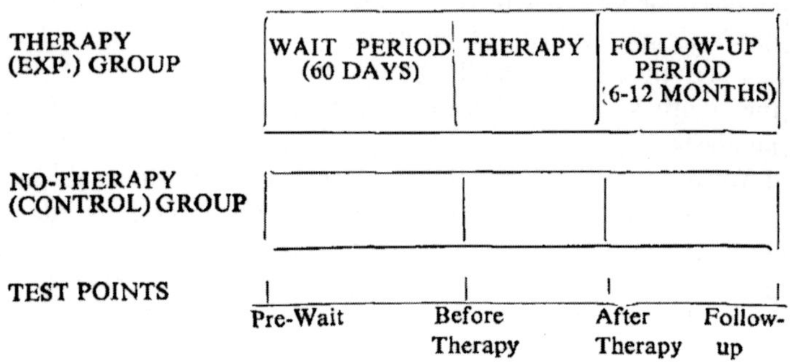

Fig. 4.1 : General Design for Study

Data on different points of test administration, including of all interviews were also collected.

Hence, after diagnosis of maladjustments in pupil-teachers through the NSQ and division of maladjusted pupil-teachers into therapy (experimental) and no-therapy (control) groups, the subjects of the therapy (experimental) group were asked to wait during a sixty day control period and then given the NSQ a second time before beginning counselling. The counselling was given individually to the every subject of the therapy (experimental) group following Rogers (1942, 1951) technique. Each interview record was noted just after the counselling ended. After the end of the therapy or after certain number of interviews when the subject felt able to solve his problems himself and he did not need help of any in this regard, then again the NSQ was administered to him to find out his adjustment status. After expiry of six months to one year of therapy, again the NSQ was given to all the subjects individually to test consistency in their adjustment.

Subjects in no-therapy (control) group were also given, at matched time intervals, the same test (the NSQ) as the therapy (experimental) group except counselling to compare its results with the therapy (experimental) group.

(iii) Analysis of Data

Analysis of data was done statistically through comparing results of therapy (experimental) group and no-therapy (control) groups, especially finding out t-value or level of confidence or different test points. The comparison of results of different test-points within the group was also done. The comparison of differences between different test-t-points mean scores of therapy (experimental) and no-therapy (control) groups was also executed.

All the calculations were carried out with the help of a mini-programmable computer, Calcom 980 model (for the programmes see Appendix—II).

Analysis of data was also done through analysing the history of each case.

CHAPTER 5

Results and Discussion

A. GROUP RESULTS : THE EXPERIMENT

(i) *Statistics of Diagnosed Maladjusted Pupil-teachers*

To identify maladjustment, if any, in pupil-teachers, the NSQ (Scheier and Cattell, 1961)—its Hindi version has been (Kapoor and Kapoor, 1974) administered to all 110 pupil-teachers of a College of Education. Table 5.1 reveals the number as well as percentage of maladjusted pupil-teachers, and it revels clearly the sex-wise ratio of number and proportion of these teachers.

TABLE 5.1

Percentage of Maladjusted Pupil-Teachers

Sex	Number of pupil-teachers participated in Test Administration	Number of maladjusted pupil-teachers identified	Percentage of Maladjusted pupil-Teachers
Males	82	28	34.15
Females	28	12	42.86
Total	110	40	36.36

Table 5.1 shows that in average 36.36 per cent of the total of 110 pupil-teachers were maladjusted 34.15% and 42.86% of 82 male and female pupil-teachers respectively were found to have been maladjusted.

(ii) *Maladjustment Scores and Sex Differences*

In order to study the magnitude of scores on different areas of maladjustment obtained by maladjusted pupil-teachers of both the sexes the raw scores were tabulated (Appendices—III and IV and calculated (Table 5.2).

The Table 5.2 indicates that there were differences between total NSQ mean scores of these two groups and also on its I component. Therefore, the differences between 5 sets of means were subjected to t-test. The t-values of 2.47 and 2.94 thus obtained were found to be significant at .01 level of confidence in respect to the NSQ component of I and total NSQ. For the rest of the components of —F, E and An. t-values of 0.58, 0.04 and 0.83 are significant.

It is evident from Table 5.2, the female maladjusted pupil teachers were higher on component I (Tender-minded, over-protected, cultured, protected, emotional, sensitive) and on total NSQ (total neuroticism level). The results indicate that there was no significant difference between the male and female maladjusted teacher-trainees with respect to the NSQ components F (Depressive, serious inhibited tendency), E (submissiveness, dependence) and An. (Anxiety). It means that male and female pupil-teachers were similarly maladjusted on these components. In other words male maladjusted pupil-teachers were significantly lower on component I (Less tender-mindedness, less over-protected, less cultured, less protected emotional sensitivity) and on total NSQ (less maladjusted or neurotics) in comparison to female maladjusted teacher trainees.

(iii) *Group Equivalence on First Scores*

To determine if groups, in spite of the matching procedure, in terms of total scores on the first administration of the NSQ, t-test of maladjusted pupil-teachers was calculated for the difference between related means of the therapy (experimental)

TABLE 5.2

Showing Means, S.Ds. and t-Values of Male and Female Pupil-Teachers

Components of NSQ	Maladjusted pupil-teachers Male N=28		Maladjusted pupil-teachers Female N=15		Mean difference	t-value	Level of significance
	Mean	*S.D.*	*Mean*	*S.D.*			
I	12.07	2.46	14.00	1.65	1.93	2.47	.01
F	11.14	2.66	11.67	2.71	0.53	0.58	N.S.*
E	15.11	2.41	15.08	2.47	0.03	0.04	N.S.
An	12.79	2.78	13.58	2.64	0.79	0.83	N.S.
Total	51.24	2.13	54.33	3.87	2.79	2.94	.01

*N.S.=Not significant.

and no therapy (control) groups. Hence it was studied first, and the magnitude of scores on different NSQ components obtained by the maladjusted teacher-trainees of both the group and their raw scores were tabulated (Appendices—V and VI) and calculated (Table 5.3).

Table 5.3 shows the means and S.Ds. of both the groups (experimental and control). The Table 5.3 reveals that the means to the two groups differ slightly on different components of the NSQ including on the total NSQ scores. Therefore, it was tested the homogeneity of the two groups by employing t-test of significance of difference between the means.

The t-values (0.14, 1.02, 0.77, 0.69 and 0.78) are not significant, therefore, it was concluded behaviour of subjects in both the groups was homogeneous. This proves that the therapy (experimental) and no-therapy (control) groups were matched well. In other words, the two groups were not significantly different, thus leads us to conclude that the therapy (experimental) and no-therapy (control) groups were equivalent with regard to first scores on the NSQ.

Further indication of equivalence of the different groups was provided by the fact that males and females did not differ significantly on first scores. It was revealed by the Table 5.4 and Table 5.5.

Table 5.4 shows that males of two groups were not significantly different on the total NSQ scores and also on its different components.

Table 5.5 indicates that females of two groups were not significantly different on all the four components of NSQ including on the total NSQ.

(iv) Change during the Wait Period

Scores obtained by experimental and control groups at before therapy (pre-therapy) test point on NSQ were tabulated (Appendices—VII and VIII and calculated (Table 5.6).

Table 5.6 shows the means, S.Ds. and t-values of before therapy test scores. The t-values (0.39, 0.81, 0.10, 1.35 and 0.93) are not significant on different component of NSQ including the total NSQ.

TABLE 5.3

The Means, S.Ds., Difference of Means and t-Values of Raw Scores of the Subjects of Both the Groups

Components of NSQ	Therapy Group *Mean*	(Exp.) N=23 *S.D.*	No-therapy (Control) Group *Mean*	N=17 *S.D.*	Mean difference	t-value	Level of confidence
I	12-70	2.44	12.59	2.43	0 11	01.4	N.S.*
F	11.91	2.76	11.06	2.38	0.85	1.02	N.S.
E	15.35	2.52	14.76	2.25	0.59	0.77	N.S.
An	12.74	3.17	13.41	2.03	0.67	0.69	N.S.
Total NSQ	52.70	2.95	51.94	3.13	0.76	0.78	N.S.

*N.S.=Not significant.

TABLE 5.4

The Means, S.Ds., and t-Values of Male Subjects of Both the Groups in NSQ

Components of NSQ	Therapy (Exp.) Group N=15		No-therapy (con.) Group N=13		Mean Difference	t-Value	Level of confidence
	Mean	*S.D.*	*Mean*	*S.D.*			
I	11.80	2.48	12.38	2.50	0.58	0.62	N.S.*
F	12.07	2.94	10.85	2.12	1.22	1.24	N.S.
E	15.47	2.53	14.69	2.29	0.78	0.85	N.S.
An	13.53	3.27	13.08	2.18	0.55	0.58	N.S.
Total NSQ	51.87	2.27	51.15	1.95	0.72	0.89	N.S.

*N.S.=Not significant.

TABLE 5.5

The Means, S.Ds., and t-Values of Female Subjects of Both the Groups on NSQ

Components of NSQ	Therapy (Exp.) Group N=8		No-therapy (Cont.) Group N=4		Mean Difference	t-Value	Level of significance
	Mean	*S.D.*	*Mean*	*S.D.*			
I	14.38	1.19	13.25	2.36	1.13	1.23	N.S.*
F	11.63	2.56	11.75	3.40	0.12	0.07	N.S.
E	15.13	2.64	15.00	2.45	0.13	0.08	N.S.
An.	13.13	3.14	14.50	1.00	1.37	0.84	N.S.
Total NSQ	54.25	3.54	54.50	5.07	0.25	0.10	N.S.

*N.S.=Not significant.

TABLE 5.6
The Means, S.Ds. and t-Values of Before Therapy Test Scores

Components of NSQ	Experimental Group N=23		Control Group Group N=17		Mean Difference	t-Value	Level of significance
	Mean	*S.D.*	*Mean*	*S.D.*			
I	12.30	2.29	12.59	2.43	0.29	0.39	N.S.*
F	11.74	2.78	11.06	2.38	0.68	0.81	N.S.
E	14 83	2.31	14.76	2.25	0.07	0.10	N.S.
An.	12.43	3.10	13.59	1.94	1.16	1.35	N.S.
Total NSQ	51.30	2.49	52.12	3.10	0.82	0.93	N.S.

*N.S.=Not significant.

A comparison of the mean NSQ scores of the therapy (experimental) wait group at the pre-wait testing time and the mean NSQ score of the matched control group that was not motivated for therapy, shows that the difference between two groups were not significant. It means that both the groups were equally poor in adjustment.

The above Table 5.6 shows that the mean NSQ score of neither these groups changes significantly over the waiting period and that the two groups remained insignificantly different at the pre-testing point. It means that the groups were equally maladjusted at the pre-testing point also.

The findings are very similar to those reported for previous test point. One marginal difference is that the small change appearing here for the therapy (experimental) group is in the direction of less maladjusted behaviour. However, there was no significant tendency for either the high or the low NSQ scores to change more than the other over the sixty-day waiting period.

The motivation of the therapy (experimental) group to improve, as evidenced from the fact that they were told that counselling or therapy would be given, was not sufficient in itself to produce a significant decrease in the NSQ score (which proves better adjustment) in the absence of therapy. The fact that there was no change in the control group's mean score over this sixtydays' period seems to show that an increase in familiarity with the test does not lead to decrease in the NSQ score (for better adjustment).

Thus only fractional changes occurred over the wait period on NSQ score, and the direction of these changes fails to support the hypothesis that subjects motivated for therapy would improve over a period of no-therapy (wait-period).

(v) *Termination Status of the Cases af Attrition Group*

Table 5.7 shows the information about termination status of the nine subjects.

The Table 5.7 describes that there were nine subjects in the attrition group. For the most part these subjects did not get treatment at all, since they broke off their therapy after an interview or two.

TABLE 5.7
Termination Status of the Subjects in the Attrition Groups

No. of subjects	No. of Interviews per subject	Reasons for Termination of Therapy
2	0	Took Pre-wait and before Therapy test but failed to show for first therapy interview.
5	1	Removed from the therapy because they left the city.
2	2	Came in more to inquire about therapy than to actually begin therapy.

Hence, the attrition group was terminated from the study and no effort was made for further elaboration of this group.

(vi) *Change during the Therapy Period as Compared to an Equivalent No-therapy Period*

Having established that subjects motivated for therapy do not change significantly over a period of no therapy, now it is compared the change of subjects during therapy with the change of the matched control during an equivalent time period of no-therapy.

Post test (After therapy) scores of Experimental (therapy) continuers group and control (no-therapy) group were tabulated (Appendices VIII and IX) and calculated (Tables 5.8, 5.9 and 5.10)

Table 5.8 shows the means and S.Ds. of experimental and control groups. To test the significance of difference between means of two groups (on different components of the NSQ and total neuroticism level) t-test was employed and the results are shown in the same table.

It is evident from the Table 5.8 that the obtained values of t 2.01, 2.11, 2.55 and 5.75 are significant at .05, .05, .01 and

TABLE 5.8

The Means, S.Ds. and t-Value of Post Test Scores

Components of NSQ	Therapy (Experimental) Group (N=14)		No-therapy (Con.) Group (N=9)		Mean Difference	t-Values.	Level of significance
	Mean	*S.D.*	*Mean*	*S.D.*			
I	10.14	2.48	12.33	2.65	2.19	2.01	.05
F	9.50	2.03	11.11	3.02	1.51	1.53	N.S.*
E	12.43	2.59	14.56	1.96	2.13	2.11	.05
An	11.07	3.17	14.00	1.66	2.93	2.55	.01
Total NSQ	43.07	3.73	52.22	3.70	9.15	5.75	.001

*N.S. =Not significant.

.001 levels of confidence for I, E, An. and total NSQ respectively. However, there was difference in scores of both the groups for *F* component also, but it was not significant. Nevertheless, these results clearly indicate that the experimental (therapy) group which went through the therapy became better adjusted than the control (no-therapy) group which was kept aloof from the therapy.

Further a comparison of experimental (therapy) group and control (no-therapy) group with regard to differences in scores between the pre-and post-therapy administration was done. The results are presented in Table 5.9.

TABLE 5.9

Comparison of Differences Between Pre-and Post-Therapy Total Scores of Experimental (Therapy) and Control (No-Therapy) Groups

	Therapy Group (Experimental)	No-therapy Group (Control)
N.	14	9
Mean Diff. (Pre-to Post-therapy) ...	9.00	0.22
S.D. Diff	1.57	0.67
		t = 15.68
		p = .001

Table 5.9 shows the differences with regard to total scores on the NSQ. The difference between the means of the two groups was statistically significant (.001 level of confidence).

Table 5.10 shows the comparison between the experimental group and the control group with regard to differences between pre-and post-therapy scores on each of the components of the NSQ.

From the results shown in Table 5.9 and 5.10 a conclusion can be drawn that there were significant changes in total scores except in Anxiety component during the therapy period. Differences were significant at the .05, .01 and .05 level of confidence on I, F and E components respectively. The

TABLE 5.10

Comparison of Differences Between Pre-and Post-Therapy Scores on Different NSQ Components of Experimental and Control Groups

NSQ components	Mean Differences between Pre-and Post-therapy Scores: Therapy Group N = 14	No-therapy Group N = 9	Level of significance
I	2.29	0	.05
F	2.93	0	.01
E	2.29	0	.05
An	2.00	0.22	N.S.*

* N.S. = Not significant

difference was not significant on Anxiety component of the NSQ. Changes occurred, but were not significant. It indicates to some extent that anxiety remains in teacher-trainees. However, in total personality adjustment, these changes were highly significant.

The results lead to the conclusion that therapy helps in better adjustment or to be mentally healthy, while absence of therapy maintains the maladjustment or neither familiarity with the test nor the passage of time has any appreciable effect on the scores of the control (no-therapy) group.

Thus the results justify the hypothesis that there would be improvement in experimental group during therapy.

An interesting sidelight showed up when the group was divided into two sex groups. Table 5.11 shows that, although both male and female members in the experimental group on the total mean scores changed significantly (.001 level of confidence) over the therapy period however, the males showed significantly greater change in favour of increased adjustment than did females (lower the NSQ score better the adjustment).

Also the difference in adjustment of the sexes as measured by this test (the NSQ), while not significant before therapy, was significant after therapy. But males were lower than females on total mean scores (lower the score better the adjustment).

TABLE 5.11

Sex Differences in NSQ (Mean) Score Changes over Therapy

Group	Therapy (Experimental)		No-therapy (control)	
	Males N=9	Females N=5	Males N=5	Females N=4
Pre-Therapy				
I	11.89	13.40	11.60	13.25
F	12.67	12.00	10.60	11.75
E	14.44	13.60	14.20	15.00
An.	12.67	13.80	14.20	14.25
Total NSQ	51.67	52.80	51.00	54.25
Post-therapy				
I	10.44	9.66	11.60	13.25
F	9.67	9.20	10.60	11.75
E	11.67	13.80	14.20	15.00
An.	10.56	12.00	14.00	14.00
Total NSQ	42.43	44.40	50.80	54.00

These sex differences did not occur in control group sample, suggesting that something in the therapy situation itself was responsible for this change.

The above results reject the hypothesis that there would be larger improvement among females than males of experimental group during therepy.

However, male members were slightly higher than their female counterparts on components I (sensitive vs tough) and F (depression vs cheerful), but these differences were not significant, and both were moderately adjusted on these components after therapy. On components E (submissive vs dominant) and An. (anxiety vs non-anxiety), male members were lower than item females, counterparts again here also the differences were not significant, but female members were submissive (E+) and male members were moderately adjusted on this component. Both male and female members were moderately adjusted on Anxiety component after therapy, but female members were more anxiety prone than their male counterparts.

(vii) Change from Pre-therapy to Follow-up

To observe whether the subjects of therapy (experimental) group change significantly or stay constant during follow-up period, the NSQ was administered to them again after expiry of six months to one year of therapy.

The follow-up scores of both the groups (experimental and control) were tabulated (Appendices-XI & XII) and calculated (Tables 5.12, 5.13, 5.14 and 5.15).

Table 5.12 shows that there is a marked difference between the follow-up test scores of the two groups. To test the significance of difference between these two means, t-test was employed and the results have been presented in the same Table.

The Table 5.12 shows that the obtained t-Value 6.36 on total NSQ is significant at .001 level of confidence. And also the mean differences was significant at .05, .01 and .05 levels of confidence on I, E and Anxiety components of the NSQ respectively. There was mean difference on F component also but it was not significant. The results clearly indicate that the subjects of experimental group scored less than the control group, which means that the experimental group was better adjusted than the control group during follow-up.

Further the comparison was done between the experimental group and the control group with regard to changes in total scores from the pre-therapy point to the follow-up point of six months to one year. The results are shown in Table 5.13.

The results shown in Table 5.13 demonstrate that there was highly significant difference between the therapy (experimental) group and no-therapy (control) group with respect to changes in total scores from pre-therapy to follow-up.

In order to determine if during this same period changes occurred in the scores of any of the components of NSQ, the experimental (therapy) group pre-therapy and follow-up scores were compared for significance of difference on each of the four components of NSQ. The summary of these comparison is given in Table 5.14.

TABLE 5.12

The Means, S.Ds. and t-Values of Follow-up Test Scores

NSQ components	Experimental Group N=9		Control Group N=14		Mean Difference	t-Value	Level of significance
	Mean	*S.D.*	*Mean*	*S.D.*			
I	14.14	2.48	12.33	2.65	2.19	2.01	.05
F	9.86	2.82	11.11	3.02	1.25	1.01	N.S.*
E	11.50	2.35	14.44	1.94	2.94	3.13	.01
An.	11.00	3.19	13.89	1.62	2.89	2.51	.05
Total							
NSQ	42.71	3.31	52.00	3.57	9.29	6.36	.001

*N.S. = Not significant

TABLE 5.13

Comparison of Differences between Pre-Therapy and Follow-up Mean Total Scores of Experimental and Control Groups

	Therapy (Experimental) Group	No-therapy (Control) Group
No. ...	14	9
Mean Difference (Pre-therapy to follow-up)	9.36	0.44
S.D. Difference... ...	1.82	0.73 t=13.94 P=.001

From the results shown in Table 5.14, it can be seen that there were significant differences between pre-therapy and follow-up scores of experimental (therapy) group on all the components. These differences were .05, .01, ,01 and .05 levels of confidence against NSQ components I, F, E and An. (Anxiety) respectively.

When one compares the results of pre-therapy to follow-up scores of the subjects with pre-therapy to post-therapy results, he would find that the differences were significant for both the results. However, there was some improvement in the subjects on Anxiety component at follow-up period because during therapy period subjects of experimental group had no significant change, but at follow-up period they changed sign-ficantly at .05 level of confidence on this component (Anxiety). Similarly, they improved in their adjustment on E component of the NSQ also from .05 level to .01 level of confidence. But the differences which were significant at .05 and .01 level of confidence on I and F components at post therapy period were similar at follow-up period.

The results reveal that the experimental group who had gone through therapy were benefited or brought changes in them in favour of better adjustment, while there was no significant difference between the mean scores of pre-therapy and

TABLE 5.14

Comparison of Pre-Therapy and Follow-up Scores for the Experimental (Therapy) Group on Each of the Components

(N=14)

NSQ components	Pre-therapy		Follow-up		Mean Difference	t-Value	Level of significance
	Mean	*S.D.*	*Mean*	*S.D.*			
I	12.43	2.44	10.14	2.48	2.29	2.46	.05
F	12.43	2.50	9.86	2.82	2.57	2.54	.01
E	14.21	2.39	11.50	2.35	2.71	3.01	.01
An.	13.07	3.12	11.00	3.19	2.07	1.74	.05

follow-up test points of control (no-therapy) group. Table 5.15 shows the position of control group.

TABLE 5.15

The Means of Pre-Therapy and Follow-up Tests Scores of Control (No-therapy) Group

NSQ Component.	Pre-therapy Mean	Follow-up Mean
I	12.33	12.33
F	11.11	11.11
E	14.56	14.44
An.	14.22	13.89
Total		
NSQ	52.44	52.00

From the above Table (5.15) it is clear that there was no significant change in control (no-therapy) group. It means that subjects in control group, being kept aloof from the therapy maintained their maladjustment as they were as pre-therapy test point or at first test administration (pre-wait test point).

Thus the significant changes occurred from pre-therapy to follow-up in experimental group and mere fractional changes in control group in the same duration confirm the hypothesis that therapy (experimental) group would show improvement in the follow-up.

B. CASE STUDIES

In the preceding pages group results have been presented. Such presentations are valuable from a factual point of view. However, they do not reflect the investigation done in totality. Case Studies tend to conceal the fact that counselling or psychotherapy is a warm, fluctuating, human relationship, no matter how statistically measurable the changes praduced.

The previous interpretation of group results, with the reports of the results on all the therapy cases, represents the horizontal slices which this account cuts down through in vertical fashion. In addition to this integrating in each individual case the various research procedures were followed so that the clinical meaning of the objective findings may become manifest.

Fourteen cases are presented here, each of which deals with a different type of problem. Two cases scored 57 to 60 on the total NSQ. Hence their sten score was 10. 55 to 56 scores were obtained by three cases, so their sten score was 9. Other three cases scored 52 to 53 and their sten score was 8, and scores of two cases were 49 to 51, hence their sten score was 7. However, all the cases had their scores above average on the first administration of the test. Thus they all were maladjusted. The age range of the counsellees was narrow: the youngest was 21 and the oldest 30.

As mentioned above, many dissimilarities in the problems of the cases interviewed have been found on the total NSQ at the first administration of the test. Therefore, the cases have been classified in four groups on the basis of severity of the problem of maladjustment :

I. Those who scored 57 to 60 (sten score 10)/2 cases

II. „ „ 55 to 56 (sten score 9)/3 „

III. „ „ 52 to 53 (sten score 8)/3 „

IV. „ „ 49 to 51 (sten score 7)/6 „

THE FOURTEEN CASES

Group—I : Those who scored 57 to 60 (sten score 10)

Case 20—Extremely maladjusted at pre-wait Test Point. Moderately adjusted at Post-and Follow-up Test Points.

Miss S.R. is twenty-two years old woman. She was pursuing her B. Ed. Degree.

She was a patient of maladjustment. Her total neuroticism level reached sten 10 on the NSQ at the first administration of the test,

Pre-wait Result

Against different components of NSQ, her sten scores were 7,9,5 and 10 on I,F,E and An. (Anxiety) respectively.

Her profile in stens on obtained scores on the NSQ at pre-wait test point with at post therapy test point is cited in Figure 5.1.

From the Figure 5.1 it is clear that at pre-wait test point she was higher on components I (over-protected, tender-minded and protected emotional sensitivity), F (depressive, inhibited, sober and serious) and An. (worried, guilty, tense, frustrated, emotionally immature and unstable), but she was average on component E (submissive vs dominant).

Before Therapy Result

There was no major change in the case 20 due to motivation for therapy when the NSQ was administered to her after expiry of waiting period of 60 days.

This case obtained 57 total score on the NSQ while it was 60 at pre-wait test point. It means that there was some change in the case during wait period. But there was no difference in her sten score because both the scores are equivalent to sten 10. However, this case had tendency to change. There was merely unit change in her sten scores for components F from sten 9 to 8 and component An. (Anxiety) from sten 10 to 9. Stens 7 and 5 for components I and E respectively were constant.

After Therapy Result

Therapy brought major changes in the personality adjustment of this case. Changes occurred in all components of NSQ scores. At the pre-wait test point her scores were 14, 16, 12, 18 and 60 (sten scores 7,9,5,10 and 10) on I,F,E, An. components and the total NSQ respectively while at post-therapy test point she scored 8,11,16,14 and 48 (stens 4,6,8,6 and 6) on I,F,E, An. components and total NSQ respectively.

The profile for her pre-wait and post therapy scores is given in Figure 5.1.

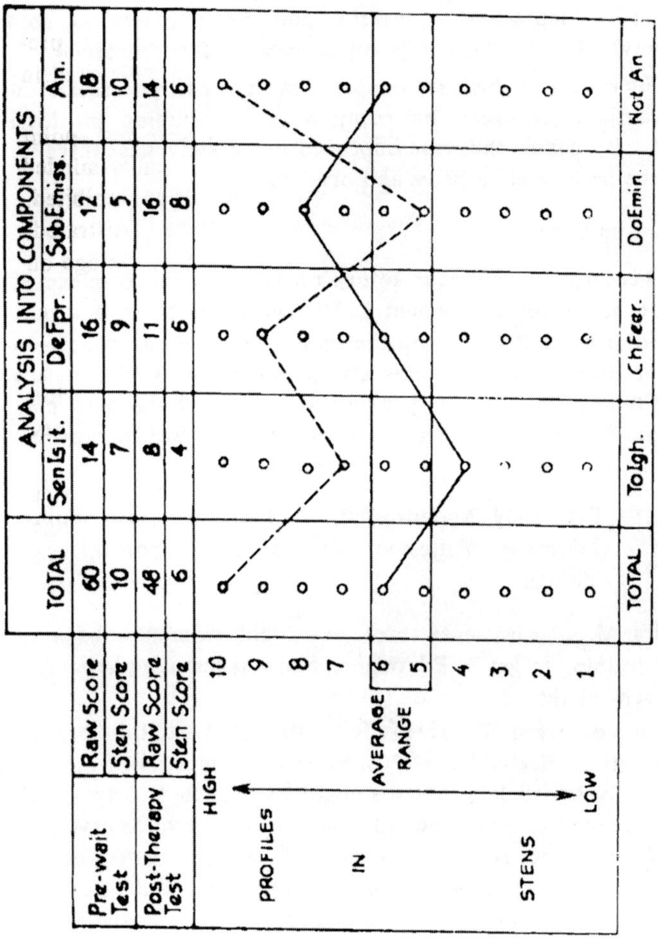

Pre-wait Scores - - - - Post-Therapy Scores ——

Fig. 5.1 : Profiles of Miss S.R.'s Pre-wait & Post-Therapy Scores on NSQ.

The Profile of post-therapy scores of this case shows that she became moderately adjusted after therapy on her total neuroticism level. However, she was lower on camponent I (self-reliant, independent and responsible), average on component F (depressive vs cheerful) and An. (Anxiety vs not-Anxiety). But she was higher on component E (submissive).

The results of this case indicate that her scores decreased on all components except on component E including on total NSQ. It means the case improved moderately after therapy. But she became submissive and obedient.

Follow-up Result

There was no change in follow-up scores of this case except in the score on component E. Her score was 16 on E at post test point while it was 15 on the same component at follow-up and it affected her sten score also (from sten 8 to 7). It means that therapy had effect on her mental health and she was able to maintain her adjustment status obtained at post-therapy test point.

Case 19—Extremely Maladjusted at Pre-Wait Test Point. Normally Adjusted at Post-and Follow-up Test Points.

Mrs. M.N. is a twenty-three years old woman. She was under training to get B. Ed. degree. She was pursuing her study to be self-reliant.

She was a divorcee. She always felt disturbed due to this because this position affected her status. Moreover allegations from the members of her society that she might be attracted to someone else disturbed her more. But she narrated that divorce gave her mental peace because she was married with a man who is illiterate, drunkard and often used to beat her and did nothing for livelihood. Her widow mother and elder brothers are sympathetic and cooperative to her and helped her in divorcing her husband and they also assist her financially in her study for B. Ed. She wanted to be a teacher first, then to be a lecturer in college to raise her lost status in her society. She remains anxious about her future.

However, she was also a severe case of maladjustment. Her total neuroticism level was highest in sten range like Case 20.

Pre-wait Result

Her pre-wait sten scores were 8,7,7,7 and 10 on I,F,E, An. components and total composite neuroticism level respectively.

Her profile in stens of pre-wait scores on NSQ is given in Figure 5.2 alongwith her profile of Post-therapy scores.

Figure 5.2 shows graphically the maladjustment status of Case 19. She was higher on components I (Sensitive and imaginative), F (depressive and pessimist), E (submissive and dependent) and An. (anxious, frustrated and emotionally immature and unstable), and on Total Neuroticism Level (extremely maladjusted).

Pre-therapy Result

There was change in positive direction in pre-therapy scores of this case. Her total score decreased from 57 to 54. Hence she reached sten 8 at pre-therapy test point while she had sten score 10 at pre-wait test point. Her scores on components I and An. also decreased at this test point and this decrease affected her sten scores.

Pre-therapy result of the case 19 indicates that she was willing to change when she was motivated for therapy.

Post-therapy Result

At post therapy test point she scored 11,9,14,13 and 47 (stens 6,5,7,6 and 6) on component I,F,E, An. and total composite Neuroticism level respectively. Her profile of scores on post-therapy test point is also shown in Figure 5.2

Figure 5.2 indicates that after therapy Case 16 was at an average range of adjustment on components I (sensitive vs tough), F (depressive vs cheerful) and An. (worried vs free from worry, tense vs calm and emotionally unstable vs emotionally stable), and also on Total Composite Neuroticism level. But she was above average on component E (submissive).

Post-therapy result of Mrs. M.N. shows that she was moderately adjusted on all components (except E component) including on total Neuroticism level on NSQ. However, she remained submissive (E+).

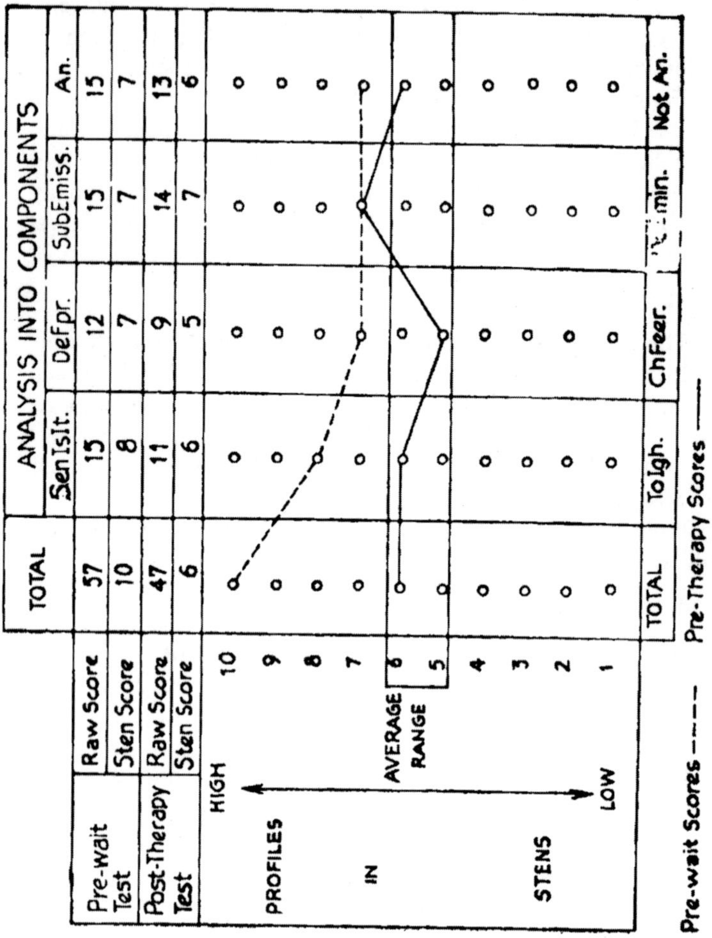

Fig. 5.2 Profiles of Miss M.N.'s Pre-Wait and Post-Therapy Scores on NSQ.

Follow-up Result

There was no change in follow-up scores of this case. It means that the scores obtained by her at follow-up test point were constant or similar to the scores at post-therapy test point. It also means that therapy helped the case to maintain her adjustment.

Group II—Those who scored 55 to 56 (sten score 9)

Case12—A serious case of Maladjustment at Pre-wait test point reached Average level of Adjustment at Post-therapy and Follow-up.

Mr. M.M. is a twenty-seven years old man. He was studying in B. Ed. class. His total neuroticism score was 56 on the first administration of the test. His score reached sten 9. Hence he was a serious case of maladjustment.

Pre-wait Result

He scored 14,10,15,17 and 56 (stens 7,6,7,9 and 9) on components I,F,E,An. and total composite Neuroticism level respectively. Profile of his pre-wait test scores is given in Figure 5.3 with the profile of Post-therapy scores.

From the Figure 5.3 it is clear that the case 12 was higher on components I (sensitive and tender minded), E (submissive and dependent) and An. (worried, tense and unstable), and also on total composite neuroticism level (highly maladjusted).

Pre-therapy Result

There was no change in pre-therapy scores of this case on any component E on which the score increased from 15 to 16 and this increase affected sten score also for this component.

Pre-therapy result indicates that motivation for therapy did not affect this case. But it helped negatively as he reached sten 8 from 7 on component E (submissive) while on other components maladjustment scores were constant or similar to the scores at pre-wait test point.

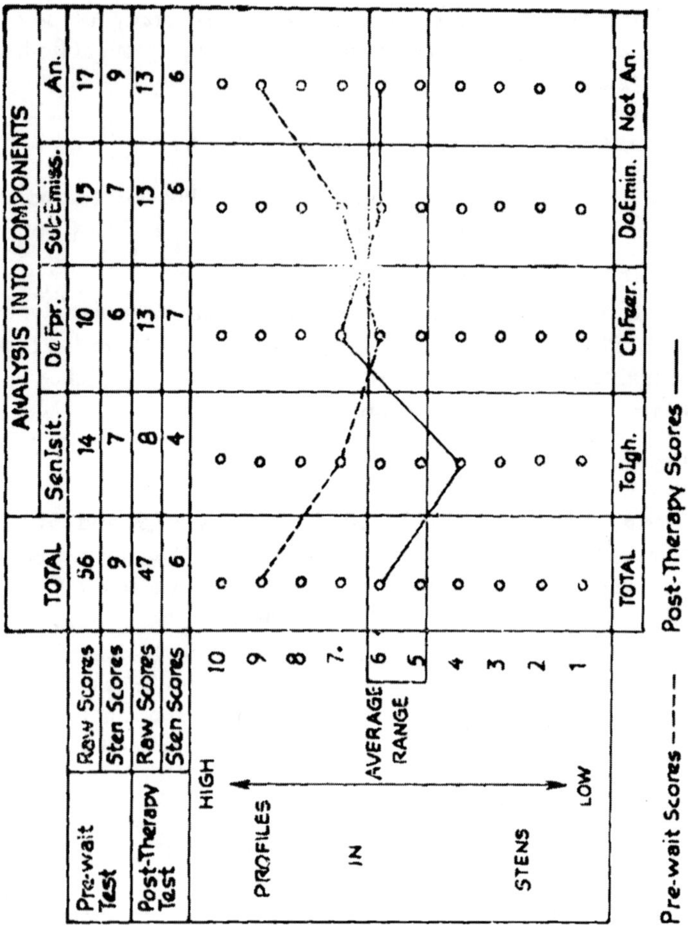

Fig. 5.3 : Profiles of Mr. M.M.'s Pre-Wait & Post-Therapy Scores on NSQ.

Post-therapy Result

This case was benefited by the therapy. His scores were decreased on all components except E including total NSQ scores at post-therapy test point. Profile of his post-therapy scores is also shown in Figure 5.3.

Figure 5.3 shows that the case 12 was lower (sten 4) on component I (tough, hard and responsible), and average (sten 6) on components E (submissive vs dominant), and An. (Anxiety vs not-Anxiety), and also on total neuroticism level. But this case was higher (sten 7) on component F (depressive and serious) after therapy. Nevertheless on total neuroticism level he was moderately adjusted.

Follow-up Result

There was no change in follow-up result. The scores on different components including total NSQ score were constant or similar to the post-therapy scores. This means that therapy had a positive effect on the case because he was able to maintain his adjustment attained during therapy.

Case 22—A serious case of Maladjustment of Higher level (sten 9) at pre-wait test point reached Average level of Adjustment at Post-therapy and Follow-up Test points.

Miss R.S. is a Twenty-five years old woman. She is in administrative job in education department and was doing B. Ed. on study leave.

She was also a serious case of maladjustment. Her total NSQ score was 56 (sten 9) on first administration of test.

Pre-wait Result

At pre-wait test point she was higher on component I (sensitive), extremely higher on component E (submissive), and total composite neuroticism level. But she was average on components F (depressive vs cheerful) and Anxiety. Her profile on pre-wait test scores with the profile on post therapy scores is given in Figure 5.4.

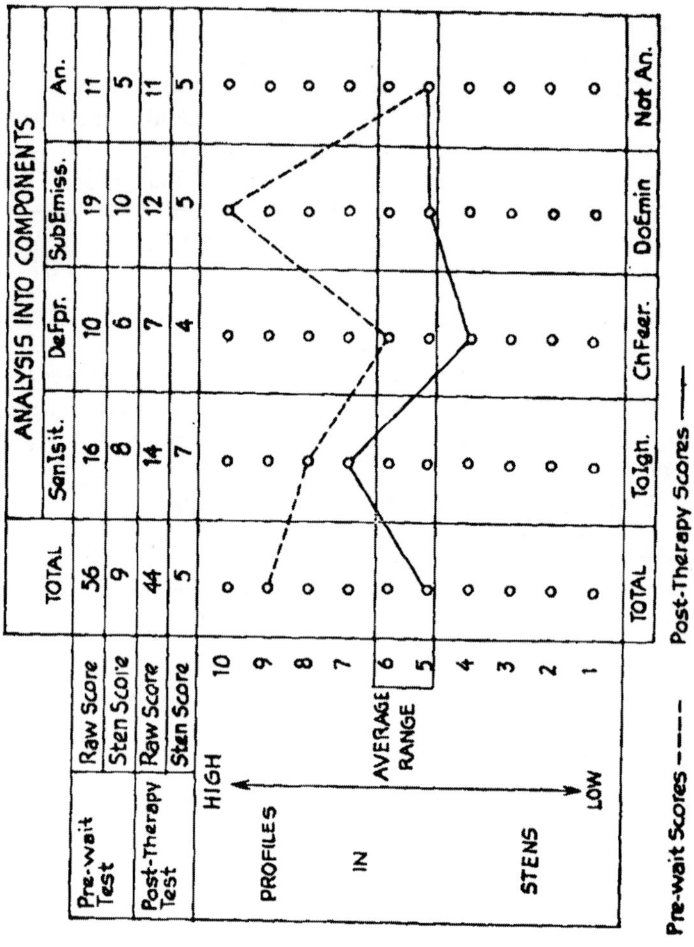

Fig. 5.4 : Profiles of Miss R.S.'s Pre-Wait & Post-Therapy scores on NSQ.

Figure 5.4 shows that the subject was extremely maladjusted because her sten score on total neuroticism level was 9 and sten 8 on component I (sensitive), sten 10 on component E (submissive). However, from this figure it is clear that she was normal on components F and Anxiety because her sten scores on these components were 6 and 5 respectively.

Pre-therapy Result

At before therapy test point this case was slightly lower than pre-wait result on components I (sensitive vs tough) and E (submissive vs dominant), and also on total neuroticism level after getting motivation for therapy. However, she was average like pre-wait test point on components F (depressive vs cheerful), An. (Anxiety vs not Anxiety). Her sten scores were 7,8 and 8 on components I,E and total neuroticism level respectively, and stens 6 and 5 for components F and An. respectively.

It means that motivation for therapy benefited this case.

After Therapy Result

This case was certainly helped by the therapy. Her maladjustment scores decreased on all components including total NSQ score except component I (sensitive) on which her score was constant or similar to the score at previous test points which was slightly higher from the average range.

Figure 5.4 also shows that the profile of her post scores which graphically describes her adjustment position after therapy.

From Figure 5.4 the adjustment status of this case is clear that she was moderately adjusted after therapy. Sten scores of this case were 4, 5, 5 and 5 on components F (cheerful) E (submissive vs dominant). An. (Anxiety vs not-Anxiety), and total neuroticism level respectively. Her sten score was 7 on component I (sensitive).

This case was benefited by the therapy on her total neuroticism level and also on other components of the NSQ either keeping herself at average range in the profile or below the average range of adjustment. However, she was remain sensitive, and therapy did not do more except maintaining her score constant on this component of I (sensitive).

Follow-up Result

At follow-up test point the adjustment status of this case was same as that of the status at post-therapy test point. There was neither increase nor decrease in the score which means the therapy had longer effect on this particular case.

Case 1—A Case of Higher Level (sten 9) of maladjustment of pre-wait Average Level (sten 6 and 5) adjustment at post and follow-up.

Mr. I.R. is a twenty-seven years old man. He is a son of a retired police Sub-inspector. He narrated his story that his father is an authoritarian and dominant and his nature is such that it terrorised even the family members. He was often terrorising the family members. He has been terrorised by his father since his very childhood. He always criticised him even when he became self-reliant by getting teaching job. He was always worried and anxious about the future of his brother and sister.

Mr. I.R. is also a serious case of higher level on NSQ at pre-wait test point. However, after therapy he became moderately adjusted and this adjustment was maintained in follow-up also.

Pre-wait Result

At pre-wait test point this case was higher on total neuroticism level, also on components F (depressive) and E (submissive) and high on component I (sensitive). But he was average on component An. (Anxiety vs not-Anxiety).

Figure 5.5 shows graphically the profile of Mr. I.R's pre-wait and post-therapy tests scores. From the profile of pre-wait test scores it is clear that his sten score on total neuroticism level was 9 and sten scores on components F and E were 8 each and on I component it is 7 while on An. component it was 5.

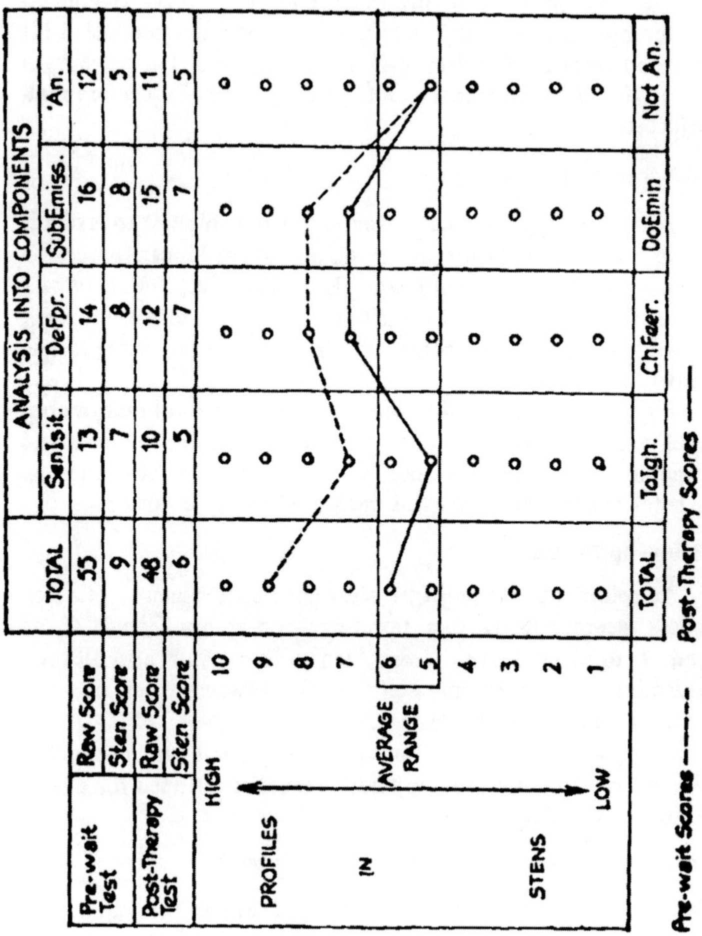

Fig. 5.5 : Profiles of Mr. I.R.'s Pre-Wait & Post-Therapy scores on NSQ.

Pre-therapy Result

There was no change in the scores of this case except in his scores of An. (Anxiety) and E (scores increased on An. and E by digit one each) during his 60 day wait period. It means that motivation for therapy did not help him to bring change on the components I and F, but this smaller change affected his score on total neuroticism level, increasing his sten score from 9 to 10. It means that wait period made him more maladjusted.

Post-therapy Result

After therapy the case I moved from highest to average range on total neuroticism level, and from higher to high on component F (depressive) and E (submissive). But he was average on components I (sensitive vs tough) and An. (Anxiety vs not Anxiety). The profile of his post therapy score is also shown in Figure 5.5.

Figure 5.5 shows that his sten score on total neuroticism level was 6. His stens on components F and E were 7 each and 5 each on components I and An. It means that after therapy on total neuroticism level this case moderately adjusted.

Follow-up Result

At follow-up test point he showed improvement. His sten scores decreased by one point each on components E (from sten 7 to 6) and An. (from sten 5 to 4) and also on total neuroticism level (from sten 6 to 5). However, stens on components I and F were constant.

It reveals the fact that therapy was effective and still operative even after the therapy had been discontinued for a long period of time.

Group III—Those who scored 53 to 54 (sten 8)

Case 15—A Case of Higher Level of Maladjustment at pre-wait test point. But he was a case of Average Level of Adjustment at post-and follow-up test points.

Mr. R.N. is a thirty years old married man. He is working as a teacher and was doing B.Ed.

He wanted to escape from the worldly affairs by becoming a *Sadhu* or a *Yogi.* To fulfil his ambition he completed *Yoga* course, and for sometime he became a teacher of Yoga by teaching and practising it. But his mind was not strict on one area of work. He was much inclined to shift his mind to change the field of activities either to serve for upliftment of the youth of his village by organising 'Yuwak Mandal' (youth club) and sports club or to raise his academic qualification by doing Ph.D. in sociology or education apart from doing teaching job in a school.

Hence, he was mentally and emotionally unstable. This was why he was a case of higher level of maladjustment scoring higher on total neuroticism level on the NSQ. But after therapy he became moderately adjusted.

Pre-wait Result

In Figure 5.6 the profile of his pre-wait and post-therapy scores on different components including on total neuroticism level is shown. From the profile of pre-test scores figure it is clear that sten scores of this case were 8 on total neuroticism level, 9 on I component, 8 on F component and 6 on E component and 4 An. component.

Thus at pre-wait test point this case was higher on total neuroticism level and also on component I (sensitive), F (depressive). However, he was average on component E (submissive vs dominant) and lower on component An. (not-Anxiety).

Pre-therapy Result

There was no change in the pre-therapy scores of this case except unit change (decreasing) on component E. It means that motivation for therapy did not help the case to be in better adjustment position in absence of therapy.

After therapy Result

Scores of this case was decreased after therapy on all components of NSQ including the total neuroticism level except the component E. Figure 5.6 also shows his profile of post-

		TOTAL	ANALYSIS INTO COMPONENTS			
			SenIsit	DeFpr	SubEmiss.	'An.
Pre-wait Test	Raw Score	54	17	14	13	10
	Sten Score	8	9	8	6	4
Post-Therapy Test	Raw Score	44	8	11	14	11
	Sten Score	5	4	6	7	5

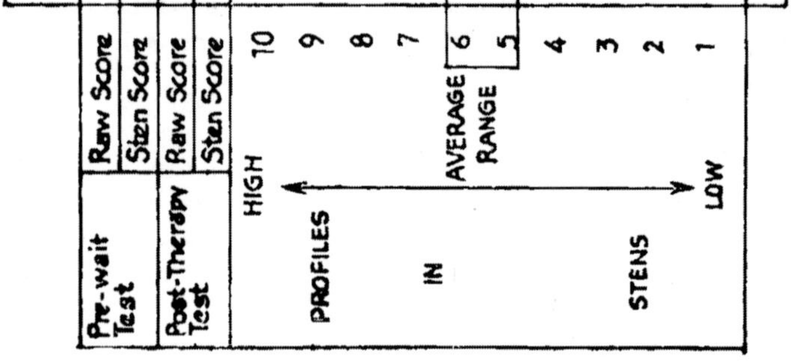

Pre-wait Scores ------ Post-Therapy Scores ——

Fig. 5.6 : Profiles of Mr. R.N.'s Pre-Wait & Post-Therapy Scores on NSQ.

scores on different components and on total composite neuroticism.

From Figure 5.6 it is also clear that the case 15's sten scores on post-therapy test point were 4, 6, 7, 5 and 5 on I, F, E. An components and total neuroticism level respectively. It means after therapy he was lower on component I (practical and responsible), average on component F (depressive vs cheerful), component An. (Anxiety vs not-Anxiety) and total composite neuroticism level. But he was higher on component E (submissive and obedient). However, he was moderately adjusted after therapy on total neuroticism level.

Follow-up Result

The follow-up scores of this case were similar to post-therapy scores. During therapy there was change in positive direction except on component E+ (submissive) and this gain was maintained through follow-up period.

Case 11—A Case of Higher Level of Maladjustment at pre-wait test point arrived at Average Level of Adjustment After-Therapy and Follow-up Test points.

Mr. R.H. is man of twenty-four years old pursuing his study for B.Ed. degree.

He had stomach trouble which was not physical. A physician who diagnosed his disease seems to have confirmed, this has to do with mental condition. In the beginning of counselling interviews he denied to have any problem either physical or mental. Gradually in further interviews he accepted that he had a failure in love affairs which created mental disturbances in him. According to his narration he was unsuccessful in his affair due to fear of his parents' prestige and social status which might go down by involving in such acts. He had fear of propaganda against him. He had no courage to face the society even if false allegations were made against him.

He was depressed and submissive, and highly maladjusted on total neuroticism level at first administration of the NSQ.

Pre-wait Result

At pre-wait test point he was higher on component F, E

and on total NSQ. But he was average on component I and lower on component An.

Figure 5.7 also shows graphically his profile of pre-wait scores on NSQ different components and also on total neuroticism level.

Mr. R.H.'s sten scores were 10 on component F, 8 on component E, 5 on component I and 4 on component An. But his sten score on total neuroticism level was 8.

At pre-wait test point he was depressive and serious (F+), submissive (E+), but moderately adjusted on I (sensitive vs tough) and he was free from anxiety (An.—). However, he was higher on total neurotism level.

Before Therapy Result

At pre-therapy test point there was no change in his scores except unit change in decreasing direction on component E from sten 8 to 7. This minor change did not affect the sten score on total neuroticism level. It means that motivation for therapy did not work effectively in this case.

Post-therapy Result

After therapy there was a major change in this case on component F. He changed moderately on E component. But his anxiety was increased. Figure 5.7 also shows the profile of Mr. R.H.'s post-therapy scores on different NSQ components including total neuroticism level.

Adjustment status of case 11 is shown graphically in Figure 5.7. Sten scores of this case were 5 on component I (sensitive vs tough), 4 on component F (cheerful), 5 on component E (submissive vs dominant), 7 on component Anxiety (increased from sten 4 to 7), and 5 on total neuroticism level.

From Figure 5.7 it is clear that after therapy this case was lower on component F (moved from sten 10 to 4), average on component E (moved from sten 7 to 5) and also on total neuroticism level. He was average also on component I (his score on this component was constant *i.e.* sten 5). But he was higher on component An. (moved from sten 4 to 7). It means that therapy helped him to be adjusted at average

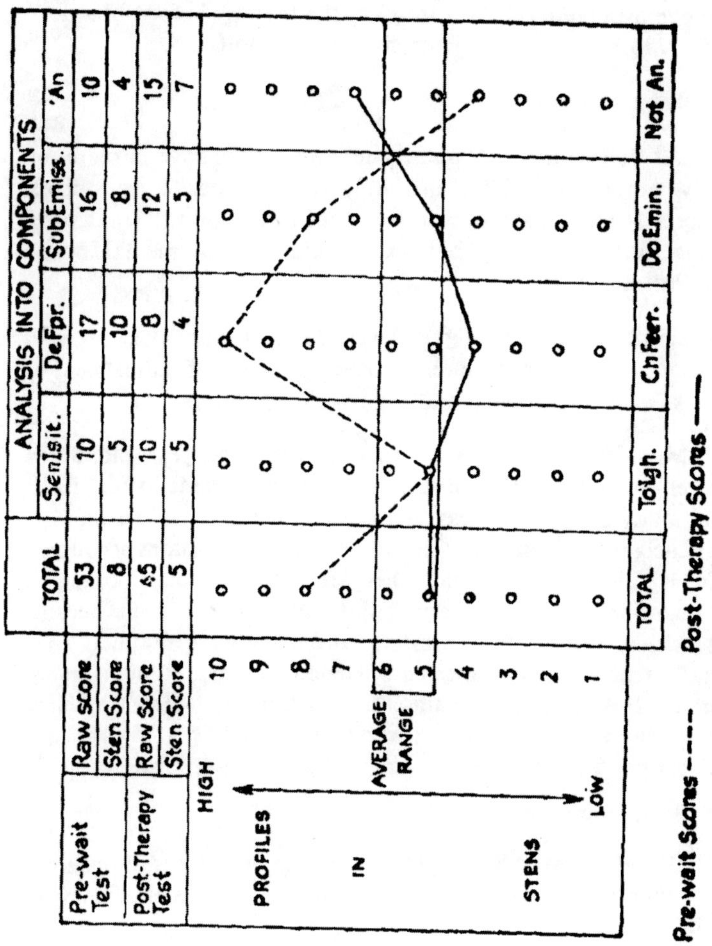

Fig. 5.7 : Profiles of Mr. R.H.'s Pre-Wait & Post-Therapy scores on NSQ.

level on components I, E and total composite neuroticism, and it led him to good adjustment on component F. But during this period his anxiety was increased and reached at above average level. Nevertheless the therapy helped him positively in his average adjustment on the whole.

Follow-up Result

At follow-up test point there was no change in scores on any component of NSQ including total composite neuroticism score. It means, scores were constant at this point. It indicates that therapy helped him to maintain his mental health (adjustment).

Case 18—A Case of Higher level of maladjustment at pre-wait become a case of Average level of adjustment at post-therapy and follow-up test points.

Miss S.P. is a frustrated woman of twenty-six years old. She is a self-made lady, discouraged by her poor parents in her efforts to study more. She was deceived by her lover. Her family's financial conditions and the boy's parents persuasions accounted for it. The promise given to her seems to have been broken by him. She developed poor adjustment in her. She became sensitive, inhibited, depressive and submissive and finally she had neurotic maladjustment. Hence she secured poor grades in her B.A. and M.A. examinations. Certainly after treatment she became normal being submissive, and secured comparatively good marks in B.Ed. and M.Ed. examinations

Pre-wait Result

Profile of Miss S.P.'s pre-wait scores on NSQ is also shown in Figure 5.8. It shows graphically the abnormal adjustment status of her.

Sten scores of this case were 7 on I component, 8 on F component, again 7 on E component, 4 on An. Component and finally 8 on total neuroticism level at pre-wait test point.

Thus this case was sensitive, kind and imaginative (I+); depressive, serious and inhibited (F+); submissive, obedient and dependent (E+). However, she was free from anxiety

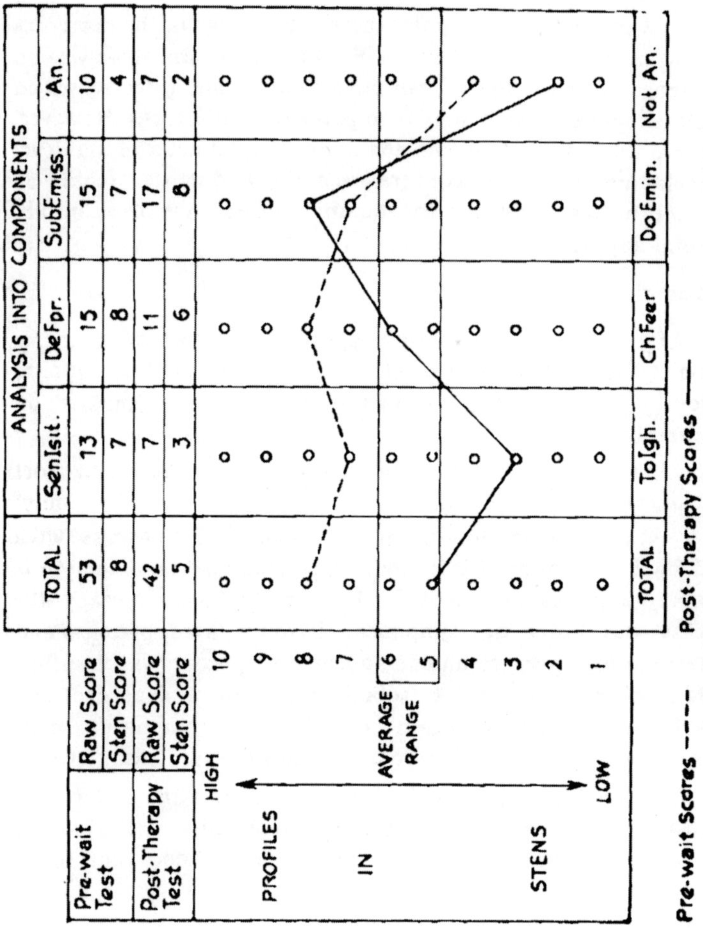

Fig. 5.8 : Profiles of Miss S.P.'s Pre-Wait & Post-Therapy Scores on NSQ.

An.—), and on the whole she was highly maladjusted (higher on total neuroticism level).

Pre-therapy Result

At pre-therapy test point there was change in the rawscores (raw score 14 for I and 14 for E) of the case. But there was no change in sten scores of respective components. (Sten scores on all components were similar to pre-wait sten scores.) However, there was (unit) change in sten score of total neuroticism level including in its raw score (raw score 51 and its sten score was 7). It means motivation for therapy affected the case in her total adjustment.

Post-therapy Result

From therapy this case was benefited by decreasing scores on different components of NSQ including total neuroticism level. However, therapy helped her to be more submissive on component E+.

Profile of her scores on different components including total NSQ is shown graphically in Figure 5.8.

At post-therapy test point sten scores of this case were 3,6.8,2 and 5 on I F E An. components and total composite neuroticism level respectively. It means that after therapy the case was lower on component I (tough, hard, practical and responsible). average on component F (depressive vs cheerful), higher on component E (submissive, obedient, dependent and soft-hearted), lower again on Anxiety component (not-Anxiety), and average on Total composite Neuroticism level.

Nevertheless therapy helped her in keeping better and healthy adjustment. However, she was submissive (E+) which is acceptable because the submissive person does not make trouble and his/her behaviour appears quite considerate, kindly, and soft-hearted.

Follow-up Result

There was no change in scores at follow-up test point of the case. It means that the follow-up scores are similar to the scores of post-therapy. It indicates that therapy was effective and it maintained the *status quo* and enabled the case to keep her adjustment healthy and normal, even after therapy was discontinued.

Group IV—Those who scored 49 to 51 (sten 7)

Case 17—A Case of high level of Maladjustment at Pre-wait reached lower level of adjustment at Post-and follow-up.

Mr. A.L. is a twenty-six years old young man. He hailed from a poor family. He is always anxious to raise the status of his parents by getting a better job. For this he toils hard, but he did not get good marks in the examination of B. Com. and M. Com. He is not encouraged by his elder uncle for his higher education. He felt insulted in such circumstances. The financial status may be called a reason responsible for it. In such situations he compares the poor status of his parents with the rich status of his uncle and suffers with relative deprivation.

Hence in the beginning he was maladjusted, but after therapy his maladjustment level decreased to below average level.

Pre-wait Result

At pre-wait test point scores of Case 17 were high or at above average level on different components of NSQ and on total neuroticism level except on component An. Figure 5.9 shows the profile of pre-wait and post therapy scores of this case on NSQ.

Sten scores of Mr. A.L. were 7 each on components I and F, 9 on component E, 3 on An. component and again 7 on total composite neuroticism level at pre-wait test.

Thus he was sensitive (I+), depressed (F+) and submissive (E+), and free from anxiety (An.—); however, his neuroticism level was high (highly maladjusted) at pre-wait test point.

Pre-therapy Result

There was no change in the scores of this case at pre-therapy test point except in the score on component E (there was unit change in its score on the positive direction). It means, motivation for therapy did not help him to bring change in his better adjustment.

Post-therapy Result

At post-therapy test point his scores on different components including total neuroticism level decreased to average and below average level.

Figure 5.9 also shows graphically the levels of adjustment of this case. His sten scores were 4 each on component I, F and total neuroticism level, and 5 on component E and 6 on An. component.

Thus after therapy this case became practical, tough, hard and responsible (I—), cheerful, happy-go-lucky (F—). But he was moderately adjusted on components E (submissive vs dominant) and An. (Anxiety vs not-Anxiety). However, he was well adjusted on total composit neuroticism level.

Follow-up Result

There was no further change in the scores of this case at follow-up test point either in positive or negative direction after the termination of therapy. It does not mean that the therapy lost its effect on the case. It, however, enabled the case to sustain his mental health even after the therapy was stopped.

Case 10—A Case of Above Average level on NSQ at pre-wait test point reached below Average on the same Test at post-therapy and follow-up test points.

Mrs. K.J. is a twenty-seven years old maladjusted woman. She comes from a middle class family. She has a keen desire for teaching and was doing B. Ed. But her in-laws were not cooperative in her mission. However, her husband was cooperative, though he also used to discourage her for not doing all household works like child-rearing, cooking, washing clothes etc., apart from her study in B. Ed. Hence she always remains in an anxious state and in a dilemma.

Nevertheless, therapy helped her in adjusting herself for a better adjustment state.

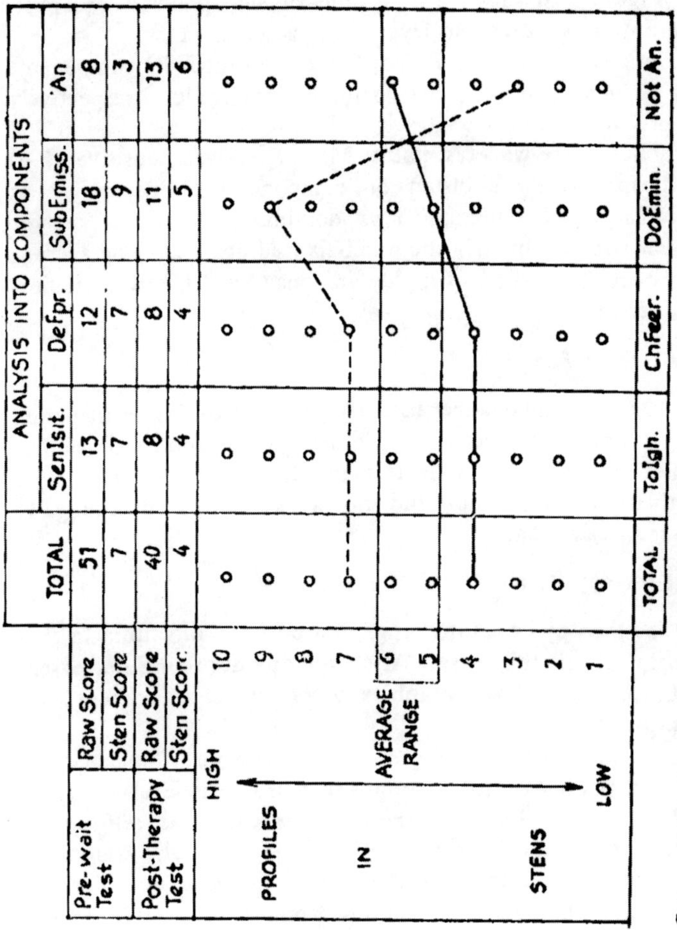

Pre-wait Scores ----- Post-Therapy Scores ——

Fig. 5.9: Profiles of Mr. A.L.'s Pre-Wait & Post-Therapy Scores on NSQ.

Pre-wait Result

At first administration of the test, her total neuroticism level was high. Her anxiety was so high and she was more sensitive.

Figure 5.10 shows the profile of her pre-wait and post-therapy tests scores and level of her adjustment.

Her sten scores were 7, 5, 5, 9 and 7 on the NSQ components I F E, An. and total composite neuroticism level respectively at pre-wait test point.

Thus at pre-wait test point Mrs. K.J. was sensitive (I+) and moderately adjusted on components F (depressive vs cheerful) and E (submissive vs dominant); however, on the latter component (E) she was balanced due to having average score on E, but she was highly anxious (An.+), and maladjusted on the whole.

Pre-therapy Result

There was no change in her adjustment during wait-period of 60 days. Her scores at pre-therapy test point were similar to her scores at pre-wait test point. It means that simply motivation for therapy did not work to bring any change in her maladjustment.

Post-therapy Result

The therapy brought change in a positive direction in the adjustment of this case. After therapy her scores decreased. Figure 5.10 also shows graphically her level of adjustment after therapy.

Her sten scores were 4 each on components I,F and E, 7 on An. and again 4 on total composite neuroticism level.

It is obvious that after therapy this case was self-reliant, independent-minded and responsible (I—), cheerful, harmonious liked social contact (F—), vigorous, forceful and decisive (E—) and well adjusted on total neuroticism level. But she was still anxious (An.+). However, her score on anxiety decreased by digit two (from sten 9 to 7). It indicates that the case tried to adjust in positive direction. On the whole her total neuroticism level was satisfactory.

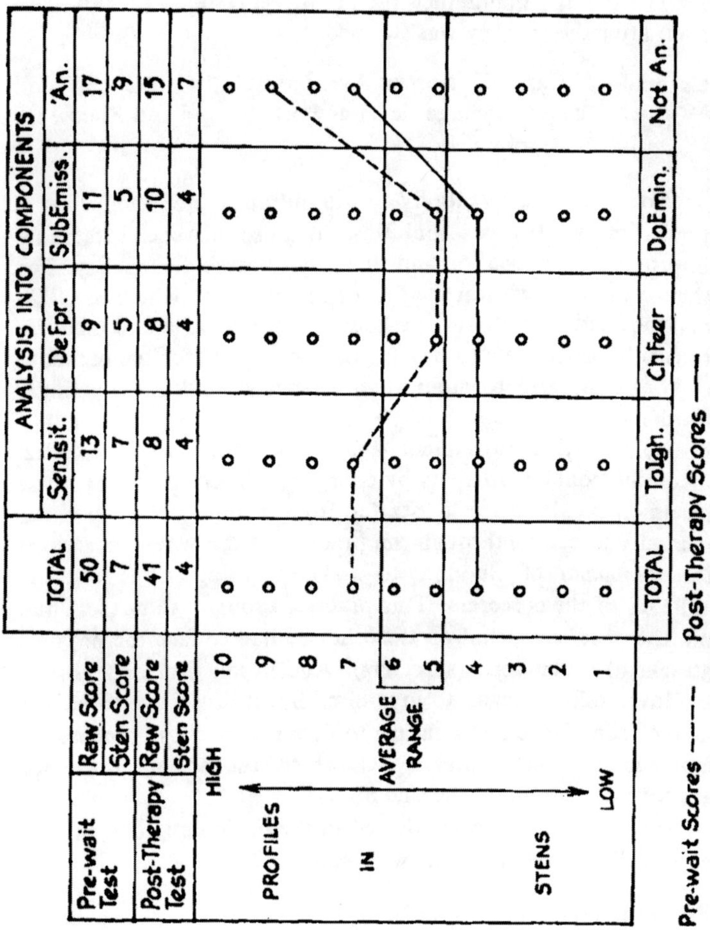

Fig 5.10 : Profiles of Mrs. K.J.'s Pre-Wait & Post-Therapy Scores on NSQ.

Follow-up Result

There was no change in the scores of this case also at follow-up test point. The follow-up scores were similar to the post-therapy scores.

The therapy maintained the adjustment status of this case even after the therapy was stopped.

Case 14—A Case of Above Average level at Pre-wait and Below Average level at Post-therapy and Follow-up Test points.

Mr. M.K. is a twenty five years old man. He belongs to a poor family. He has ambition to raise his social status by improving his education and there by to serve the society. For this he used to perform the job of his parents' which is *Bidi*-making and sometimes he had to become a manual labourer to earn more money to pay for tuition fee and for the purchase of books and also to support his parents and four younger brothers.

He started a movement against sorcerers who exploited mentally troubled villagers by charging a heavy free for their treatment. He himself started to do this job of treating mentally ill people through the practice of the ways prescribed in *Dhampada* of Buddha to make the villagers free from the clutches of the sorcerers. This practice brought fame for him on the one side, but on the other he had to face the physical attacks of his enemies (sorcerers). And in this process a girl of a Govt. officer began to love him. But it failed due to having lack of confidence and courage to face the society because of his socially unacceptable act which the society does not approve and so might defame him.

However, he was maladjusted in the beginning, but in due course of treatment he was well adjusted.

Pre-wait Result

At pre-wait test point he was normal (average) on three components of the NSQ while anxiety was higher and total maladjustment was high in him.

Profiles of his pre-wait post-therapy scores are shown in

Figure 5.11 which shows graphically maladjustment and adjustment status of this case.

Sten scores of this case were 6 each on components I, F E ; 8 on An. and 7 on total neuroticism level at pre-wait test point.

Thus he was average on I (sensitive vs tough), F (depressive vs cheerful) and E (submissive vs dominant), and he was above average on An. (Anxiety) and total neuroticism level. It means that at pre-wait test point this case was anxious and on total he was highly maladjusted.

Pre-therapy Result

There was no change in total NSQ score of this case but there was change on both the directions (positive and negative) on the components at pre-therapy test point.

His sten scores decreased from 6 to 5 and 8 to 7 on the components I and An. (Anxiety) respectively. But his sten score increased from 6 to 7 on component E. However, his sten score was constant (*i.e.* 6) on component F and total neuroticism level (*i.e.* sten 7).

Thus at pre-therapy test point this case was moderately adjusted on components I (sensitive vs tough) and F (depressive vs cheerful), but he was submissive (E+), anxious (An.+) and highly maladjusted on total neuroticism level.

During 60 days wait period this case changed in both directions on different components of NSQ keeping his adjustment constant on a certain component and also on total neuroticism level.

Post-therapy Result

Therapy decreased the scores of this case leading to better adjustment. However, his score was slightly high (above average) on component I. It means that after therapy he became sensitive and kind while he was in between (at average level) sensitiveness and toughness before therapy and pre-wait period. However, he was average on component F (depressive vs cheerful) maintaining his adjustment level of pre-therapy period. He was lower on component E (dominant) and total

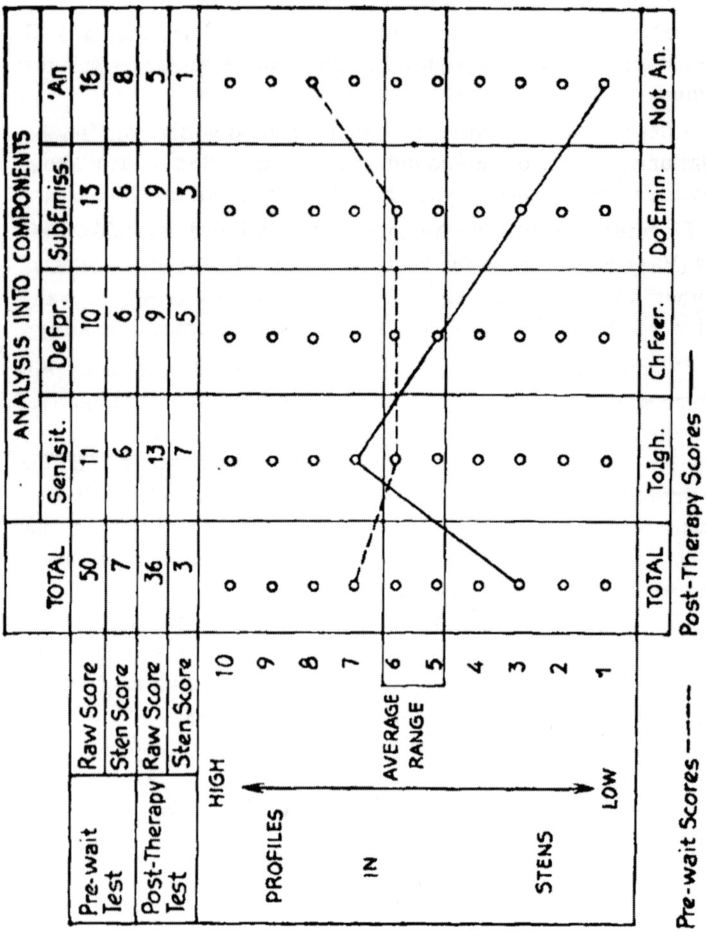

Fig. 5.11 : Profiles of Mr. M.K.'s Pre-Wait & Post-Therapy Scores on NSQ.

composite neuroticism level, and he was lowest on Anxiety component.

Figure 5.11 also shows the levels of adjustment of this case on different NSQ components. His sten scores were 7 on component I, 5 on component F, 3 on component E, 1 on An. component and 3 on total composite neuroticism level.

After therapy Mr. M.K. became emotionally mature, secure, calm and composed, self-confident, realistic, stable, resilient, and, in a broad sense, psychologically healthy (An.—).

He was vigorous, decisive, independent-minded and self-assured (E—). However, he was sensitive and kind (I+) also. He was neither so serious and depressed nor so cheerful (F+), he was balanced in this regard. Over all he became mentally healthy or well-adjusted securing total neuroticism score quite low (sten 3).

Follow-up Result

Scores of this case were constant on all components including on total NSQ score at follow-up test point. This nature of no change in scores indicates the positive effect of the therapy on the case. Even after a long gap of terminating of the therapy, the case was able to maintain his mental health or his better adjustment.

Case 5 – A Case of High Maladjustment at Pre-wait Test Point and Average Adjustment at Post-therapy and Follow-up Test Points.

Mr. V.G. is a twenty-four years old maladjusted man. He was doing B. Ed. to become a teacher in a school.

He was a good student academically during school life. So he obtained good marks in school examination. But he got poor division in P.U.C. and B.Sc. due to being anxious and pessimistic in nature. He developed this temperament because of the family burden of his parents. He had to pay loan of his parents and for this he has to say harsh words to them for not managing well the expenditure of the house. But after that he had to repent for his saying that he should not have said like this. He has anxiety of marriage of his sisters also being elder son and economically supporting member in the family.

He remained always in indecision. He got a temporary assignment of teachership in a school. But he always thought whether he would be absorbed as a permanent member of the school or not while the headmaster assured him to confirm his post.

He had doubts in everything. He always imagined what others thought of him. He had to hear hard words of others also and did not react due to fear that people might say something more bad which might insult him much, and degrade his family status. So he always retreated and withdrew his views because of fear of dispute and defame.

He wants to do M.Sc. in Mathematics privately to raise his educational status but he has doubt whether he would succeed or not.

He has attraction towards girls and imagination of this resulted in nocturnal emissions. He saw snakes and rivers in dreams usually.

After therapy he was free from his inhibition and anxiety and he became adjusted moderately. Hence he secured good marks in B.Ed. examination.

Pre-wait Result

At the first administration of the test, this case was maladjusted on total NSQ score level. At this stage his anxiety was on higher level and his depression level was also high.

Adjustment levels of this case on different components including total neuroticism are also shown graphically in Figure 5.12, on the basis of his pre-wait and post-therapy tests scores.

His sten scores were 5 on component I, 7 on component F, 4 on component E, 8 on component An. and 7 on total neuroticism level.

Thus he was moderately adjusted on I (sensitive vs tough) : however, he was serious, pessimistic, upset, restless, unable to accept and adapt to situations, has tendency to withdrawal from others and slow to move (F+) ; aggressive, competitive, extrapunitive-hostility against others (E—) ; anxious-guilty,

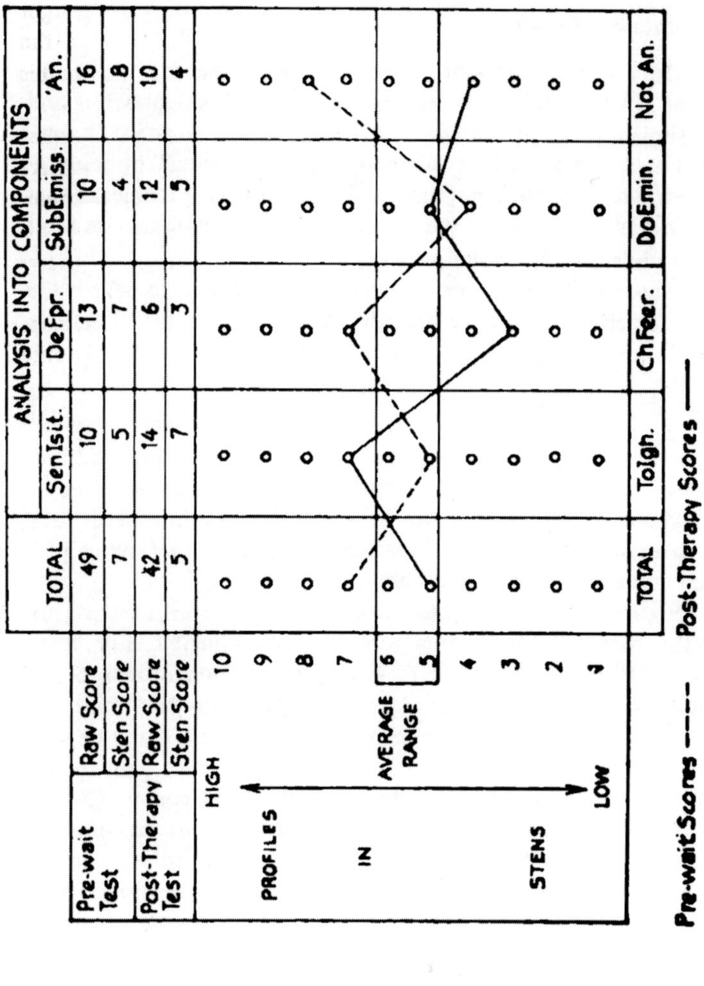

Fig. 5.12 : Profiles of Mr. V.G.'s Pre-Wait & Post-Therapy Scores on NSQ.

frustrated, lone, upset, tense, excited, restless, irritated, emotionally immatured and unstable (An. +) and maladjusted on total neuroticism level.

Pre-therapy Result

During 60 days wait-period anxiety of this case was minimised (from higher to average level), but his depression and pessimism (F+) increased. However, he was constant (balanced) on I component (sensitive vs tough) and constant being at below average on component E (dominant). It means that there was no change in the scores on I and E and also on total neuroticism level (maladjusted).

Nevertheless, perhaps motivation for therapy impelled the case for change. But he brought change in both the directions of his adjustment.

Post-therapy Result

The therapy helped the case in attaining average adjustment. His scores were decreased in the direction of good adjustment. However, score on a component increased, but in direction of balanced adjustment. Certainly therapy helped him to be sentimental and emotional.

Figure 5.12 also gives the clear ideal of adjustment status of this case. His Sten scores were 7 on component 1, 3 on component F, 5 on component E, 4 Anxiety component and 5 on total composite neuroticism level at post-therapy test point.

On the basis of the above scores after therapy he was sentimental, kind and cultured (I+) ; cheerful, humorous, enthusiastic and likes excitment and social contact (F—) ; moderately adjusted on E (submissive vs dominant—middle values sten 5 or 6 are indicative to good adjustment—balanced in both the temperament) ; but he became anxiety free, emotionally matured, calm and composed, self-confident, realistic and stable (An.—), and on total composite neuroticism level he was balanced in his adjustment.

Follow-up Result

The scores were constant at follow-up test point and similar to the scores at post-therapy test point of the Case 5,

Hence there was no change in the adjustment status of the case. In the absence of therapy, there was no increasement or decreasement in the scores. Scores at this test point being constant or being similar of post-therapy scores, indicate therapy had value and effect on maintaining adjustment of the case.

Case 7 – A Case of High Maladjusted at pre-wait and well-adjusted at post-and Follow-up.

Mr. Y.T. is a man of twenty-one years old. He was doing B. Ed. for teachership and for maintaining the economic status of the family of his parents. He has five younger brothers to support his father in their maintenance. He was much worried about family situations. And due to this his thinking became much alienating and leaving to all responsibilities by giving up his home.

His scholastic achievements were very poor due to unfavourable circumstances in the home. After joining in M.A. class he left to appear in the examination. He uses to wander in search of job for paying tuition fee and supporting the other members of his family.

At the first administration of test, he was diagnosed as maladjusted on the total neuroticism level. But he was highly depressed and submissive.

However, after therapy he became normal and well adjusted and improved his academic achievement by securing first division in B. Ed. examination.

Pre-wait Result

This case scored high on components F and E, and on total composite neuroticism level at pre-wait test point.

Profile of his pre-wait scores is also shown in Figure 5.13. It shown graphically the levels of his adjustment.

This figure shows that the case was higher on F (sten 8), E (sten 8) and total composite neuroticism level (sten 7) ; lower on I (sten 3), and average on Anxiety (sten 5). This means he was pessimistic, seclusive, retiring, unable to accept and adapt situations (F+), submissive, dependent-a milk—toast type (E+), and on the whole he was maladjusted (total NSQ level) ;

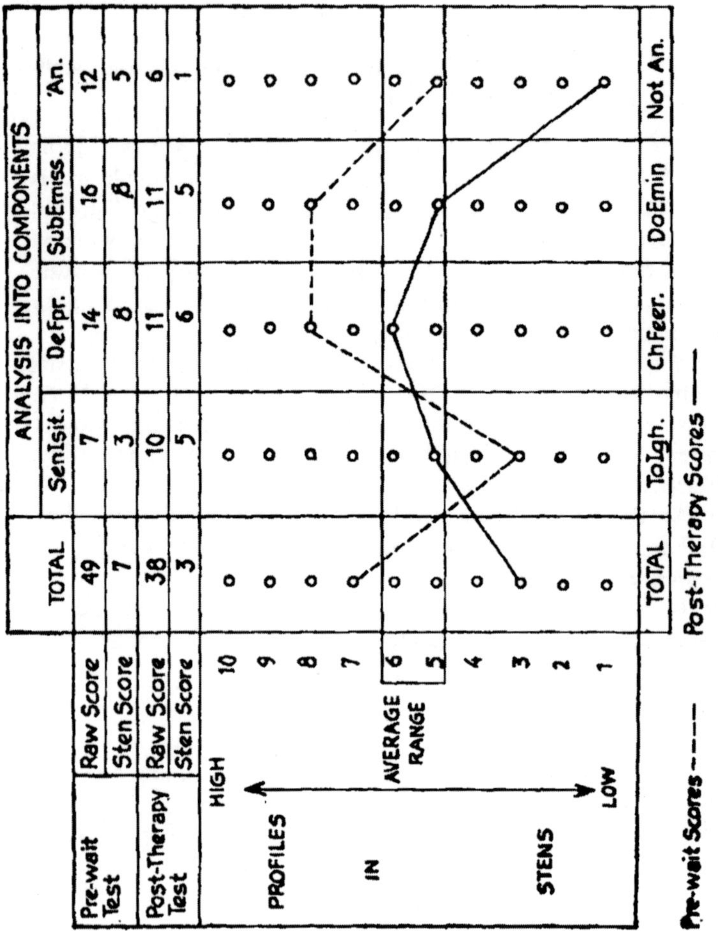

Fig. 5.13 : Profiles of Mr. Y.T.'s Pre-Wait & Post-Therapy Scores on NSQ.

however, he was practical, tough, hard and responsible (I—), and balanced in anxiety.

Pre-therapy Result

At pre-therapy test point there was no change in the scores of this case. The scores were constant. Motivation for therapy did not work for this case to bring any change in his adjustment of any side.

Post-Therapy Result

Profile or Mr. Y.T.'s post-scores is also shown in Figure 5.13. This figure shows the levels of his adjustment on different components of NSQ.

His sten scores were 5,6,5,1, and 3 on components I,F,E, An. and total composite neuroticism level respectively. He was average on I,F and E components of NSQ. He was lower (extremely below average) on Anxiety component, and lower (below average) on total neuroticism level. This means he was neither more sensitive nor more tough or hard, but he was balanced in both the temperaments (sensitive vs tough-I) neither much depressed (serious) nor much cheerful, but he was ambivalent in both the nature (depressive vs cheerful-F) ; neither over submissive nor over dominant, but he moved towards middle value (indicative to mental health) from the highly extreme value (submissive vs dominant-E) both extremes of score on this component are substantially associated with disorder. He became free from anxiety'l feelings and symptoms. Hence he was emotionally matured, secure, calm and composed, self-confident, realistic and stable (Anxiety—). On the total neuroticism level he became well adjusted or mentally healthy.

Follow-up Result

During follow-up period there was no change in the scores of this case NSQ. Scores were similar to the scores of post-therapy test point except unit change in sten on component E. This change did move the case either towards above average level or towards below average level. It means it did not affect the adjustment of the case. Nevertheless, therapy maintained the mental health of the case even after the therapy was terminated.

Case 13 – A Case of high Maladjustment at pre-wait and better Adjustment at Post-and follow-up.

Mr. H.H. is a twenty-six years old man. He was one of maladjusted teacher-trainees. He was doing B.Ed for his livelihood.

He was migrated from Bangla Desh along with his parents and other members of the family. The family of his parents was rehabilitated at Chandrapur 18 years ago. His father expired in 1982. Hence the responsibility of the house came to his shoulders being the adult male member in the family. He has four sisters (two elder from him) and two brothers. One elder sister was married. His number is third among brothers and sisters. Before joining in B. Ed. class he had to do teachership for 3 years in a local school on a temporary basis. During B. Ed. study he had to do tuition work for arranging money to pay college fee and to meet other home expenses.

He was in indecisiveness whether he should go in teaching job or in any other administrative post. In his indecision he accepted a job of Insurance Inspector after doing B. Ed. in a high good second class. But he had no job satisfaction in the Insurance Company. So he took admission in M. Ed to raise his academic qualification for getting job in teaching line.

At the first administration of the NSQ his level of maladjustment was high and he was more sentimental. But he improved his adjustment after therapy and maintained his mental health even after therapy was closed.

Pre-wait Result

Mr. H.H.'s scores of pre-wait test point also put and drawn in Figure 5.14. This figure shows the adjustment level of this case. At this point his sten scores were 7 on component I, 5 on component F, 6 each on components E and An. and 7 on total composite neuroticism level. It means at pre-wait test

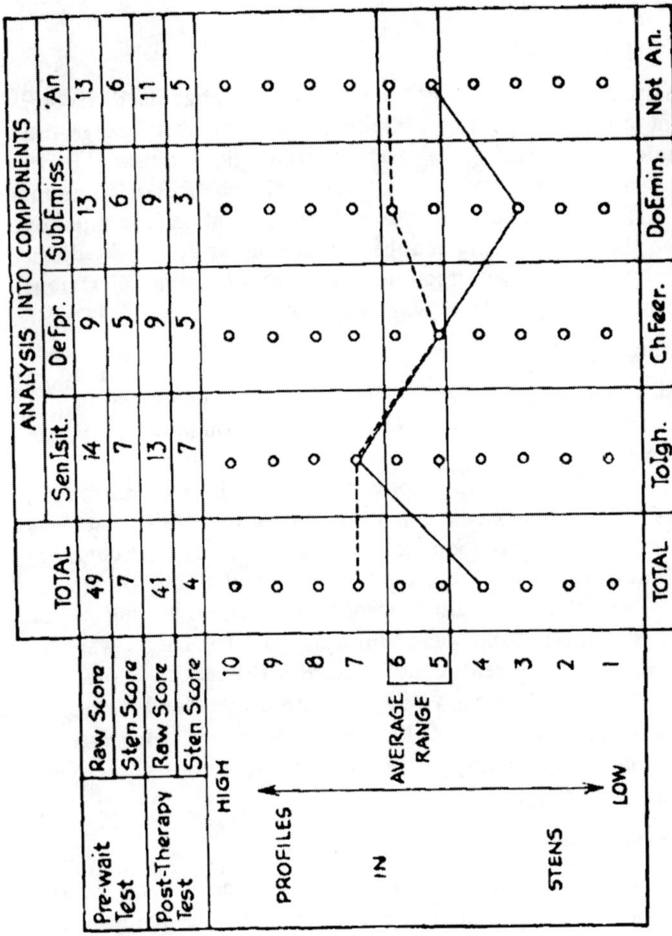

Pre-wait Scores ----- Post-Therapy Scores ——

Fig. 5.14 : Profiles of Mr. H.H.'s Pre-Wait & Post-Therapy Scores on NSQ.

point he was sentimental, kind, imaginative and fanciful (I+). He was neither depressive, nor cheerful, but he was a mixture of both (F±). He was neither submissive nor dominant, but he was balanced in both the traits (E±). He was normal in his anxiety (An.±) also. But he was not mentally healthy on his total adjustment.

Pre-therapy Result

At pre-therapy test point there was no change in the scores except unit change on component I. But this change did not affect in increasing the level of total neuroticism. However, this change increased the level of the particular component *i.e.* I+ (sensitive). It means that motivation for therapy helped the case to bring change in a particular area of adjustment, but in negative direction. However, his maladjustment on total neuroticism level was constant.

Post-therapy Result

At post-therapy test point his scores were decreased on all components including total NSQ except on component F where score was constant.

Profile of post-therapy scores of this case is also shown in Figure 5.14. It is evident from this figure that this case was higher (sten 7) on component I average (sten 5) on components F and An., lower (sten 3) on component E and also lower (sten 4) on total composite neuroticism level. This means he was sentimental, kind and cultured (I+). There was no improvement in his sentimental nature. He became dominant (E±). He was balanced in his depressive and cheerful nature (F±) and also in his anxiety (An. ±). However, he became mentally healthy (well-adjusted) on total neuroticism level after therapy.

Follow-up Result

During follow-up period there was no change in any direction in the adjustment of the case. At this point scores were constant. It means that therapy maintained the *status quo* of the mental health of the case even after its termination in assisting him for keeping good adjustment.

In brief, from the analysis of all individual cases it can be concluded that cases (*e.g.* 7,10,13,14 and 17) who scored 49 to 51 and reached sten 7 at pre-wait test point did not improve during 60 days wait-period. It means that there was no effect of motivation for therapy on these cases. However, they scored 36 to 41 and arrive at stens 3 and 4 after therapy and in follow-up. It means these five cases became well adjusted during therapy and they were able to maintain their adjustment status in the follow-up. But cases (1,5,11,12,15,18,19,20 and 22) who scored 53 to 60 and attained stens 8 to 10 at pre-wait point, some of them (cases 1,5,18,19 and 22) improved during 60 days wait period which means motivation for therapy probably affected these cases. Nevertheless, these cases scored 42 to 48 which means they reached stens 5 to 6 after therapy and in the follow-up. Thus these cases at these test points were moderately adjusted.

C. DISCUSSION

The results of this study indicate that the incidence of maladjustment in the teaching-community is very much similar to the findings of researches done by Townsend (1933), Altman (1941), Fenton (1943), Bentz Hollister and Edgerton (1971) and Ahuja (1975).

The findings regarding nature and degree of maladjustment in teachers and pupil-teachers and also sex differences in poor adjustments of this sample are akin to the researches conducted by Parashar (1961), Sharma (1963), Bina (1964), Paul (1968), Raina (1968, 1969), Gallop (1970), Gupta and Singhal (1971), Prasad (1972) and Ahuja (1975). However, their findings showed conditions and other factors responsible for these maladjustments in teachers and teacher-trainees while the present study had no concern with the causation of this problem.

The results on psycho-diagnosis and psycho-therapy of maladjusted pupil-teachers at different test points revealed that there was no significant change in therapy group over wait-period, but there was significant change in experimental group during therapy and in the follow-up, and also male pupil-teachers showed larger improvements than their female counterparts during therapy. Since there are no previous references available on comparing the results of diagnosis and therapy of maladjusted pupil-teachers, no study can be cited here in support of or in contradiction to the results obtained in the present study. However, an effort is made to discuss the results by comparing the findings of the studies done, not on maladjusted teachers or pupil-teachers, but on maladjusted and moderately maladjusted students and non-students who visited the counselling centre of the University of Chicago (USA) for their therapy and volunteered for serving as subjects for a 'research on personality'. The client-centered counselling is practised for treating the maladjusted at this centre.

In the present study it was found that there was no significant difference between the scores of experimental and control group over the period of no therapy (wait-period). This result was very similar to the findings of Gordon and Cartwright (1954) who found that no significant change (p >. 10) in the attitudes of clients occurred during the wait-period ; Rogers (1954) whose results indicate that clients during a period of no-therapy showed no significant change ; Grummon (1954) who found that there was no significant tendency for either the high or low emotional maturity scores to change more than the other over the sixty day wait-period ; and Dymond (1954) who also found that maladjustment score of neither experimental nor control group changes significantly over the waiting period. But Rudikoff (1954) found in a comparative study of the changes in concepts that the self-concept disclosed somewhat decreased adjustment over the control period (wait-period).

In the present study experimental group improved highly significantly (.001 level of confidence) during therapy. This result is supported by the findings of Butler and Haigh (1954) who found that by the end of counselling the discrepancy between self and ideal had increased for majority of clients and the mean correlation was .34 ; Rudikoff (1954) who found a very significant improvement over therapy ; Dymond (1954) who found significant increase in experimental group at post therapy ; Rogers (1954) found significant changes (.05 level of confidence) from pre to post-therapy. But findings of Grummon and John (1954) indicate that the clients with either neurotic or psychotic features in their personality show improvemant over the therapy-period. But experimental group did not show significant improvement over the therapy period. Gordon and Cartwright (1954) also found no significant changes ($p > .10$) in total scores of sub-scale scores during the therapy-period.

In the present study male as well as female teacher-trainees in experimental group improved significantly of this group improved more than their female counterparts. The results supported by Dymond (1954) who found in his study that both male as well as females respondents in experimental group changed significantly at 1 per cent level over the therapy-period. But his findings contradict the later part of the results of the present study, because in his study females showed significantly larger change in favour of increased adjustment than the males.

In the present study there was significant change in the scores of pre-therapy to follow-up. This is supported by Butler and Haigh (1954) whose finding was that a comparison of the self-ideal discrepancy of the clients at the pre-counselling point and at follow-up point indicated a statistically significant change ; Rogers (1954) whose findings also indicate that the changes from pre-therapy to follow-up were significant at 5 per cent level ; Grummon and John (1954) who found significant gains over the pre-therapy to follow-up period. Dymond (1954) found that the follow-up mean score of therapy group almost identical with the mean score at post therapy seems to indicate some lasting improvement. But the present result was contradicted by the findings of Rudikoff (1953) who found a slight loss in changes in concepts over follow-up, and Gordon and Cartwright (1954) who found that there was no significant difference ($p > .10$) between the experimental and control group with respect to changes in total scores and sub-scales scores from pre-therapy to follow-up.

The inference regarding the particular cases 7,10,13,14 and 17 who achieved better adjustment and the cases 1,5,11,12,15, 18,19,20 and 22 who became moderately adjusted after-therapy and in the follow-up is proved on the basis of the result of this experiment in its own right.

CHAPTER

Summary and Conclusions

A. SUMMARY

The development of adequate personality in all those who will teach children is the primary purpose of teacher-training. Hence an attempt has been made to identify maladjustment in pupil-teachers and to give them therapy. Before eradicating this problem of maladjustment in pupil-teachers by applying a proper therapy, it should be properly diagnosed with the help of an appropriate tool.

The rationale for selecting this problem has also been justified on the basis of a brief review of related studies which indicates that little exact research has been done to elucidate the complexities of the influence of the personalities and actions of teachers on children and there is a serious lack of research on the solution of the problem. The seriousness of the maladjusted teachers who affect learning and mental health of the pupils has also established its need to study and offer solution to the problem.

To achieve the major goal the following objectives were framed :

1. To identify maladjusted pupil-teachers.
2. To find out sex-wise proportion of maladjusted pupil-teachers.
3. To give them therapy for their better adjustment.
4. To observe the changes that have occurred in maladjusted pupil-teachers during wait, therapy and follow-up periods.
5. To popularize the utility of methodology employed in the study if it succeeds.

Keeping in view the above objectives the following hypotheses were formulated :

1. Subjects motivated for therapy will improve over a period of no therapy (wait period).
2. There will be improvement in experiment group during therapy.
3. There will be larger improvement in females than males of experimental group during therapy.
4. Therapy group will show improvement in the follow-up.

To start to study maladjustment in pupil-teachers a preliminary try-out was conducted on a small sample (N=14) of secondary teacher-educators of a College of Education by administering Neuroticism Scale Questionnaire (The NSQ). After ascertaining the sensitivity of the test (The NSQ) and finding it to be suitable in respect of its unambiguity ; time for its administration and acceptability it was administered on 110 pupil-teachers. Of them 40 pupil-teachers were identified as maladjusted and considered subjects for the study. They were divided stratifically and proportionately into two groups—experimental (therapy) and control (no-therapy).

The subjects of both the groups were tested at four test points. The subjects of experimental group were asked to wait during a sixty day control period and then given the NSQ a second time before the beginning the therapy. Then therapy was given individually to every subject of the experimental group following Rogers' non-directive technique of therapy. Each interview record was noted just after the counselling (therapy) ended.

After the end of the therapy or after certain number of interviews when the subjects felt confident to solve their problems themselves and they did not need help from anyone in this regard, then again the NSQ was administered to them to find out their adjustment level. After expiry of six months to one year of therapy, again the NSQ was given to all the subjects individually to test consistency in their adjustment.

Subjects in control (No-therapy) group were also given, at matched time intervals, the same test (The NSQ) as the experimental group except therapy to compare its results with the experimental group.

Percentage and t-test statistics were used in interpreting the data. Every individual was also analysed in Case-Study and also through the analysis of profiles of each case's scores on NSQ.

The results of this experiment have shown that the experimental group which was given therapy improved significantly and the control group which was kept aloof from therapy maintained its maladjustment.

On the basis of the results, it was possible to arrive at certain conclusions and to make some suggestions for further study in this field.

B. CONCLUSIONS

Statistical analysis of the data as well as analysis of individual cases and discussions thereupon provide the following conclusions :

1. Out of 110 pupil-teachers 36.36 per cent were maladjusted. Percentage of male maladjusted pupil-teachers was 34.15 out of 82 pupil-teachers while 42.86 per cent female pupil-teachers were maladjusted out of 28 female teacher-trainees.
2. At pre-wait test point both the groups—experimental and control—were equally maladjusted.
3. Out of four components only one component *i.e.* I and total composite neuroticism level differentiate male pupil-teachers from the female pupil-teachers other-

wise both the sexes on other components (F, E and An.) were equally maladjusted before therapy.

4. Female maladjusted pupil-teachers were more tender, emotionally sensitive and over-protected (I+) and overall more neurotic than their male counterparts. However, both were equally depressive and serious (F+), submissive and dependent (E+), and anxious (An.+) before therapy.
5. There was no significant improvement in experimental group during the wait period, and also there was no significant change in scores of control group during this period.
6. Experimental group improved significantly (.001 level of confidence) during therapy while there was no improvement in control group due to absence of therapy.
7. After therapy experimental group improved significantly .05, .01 and .05 level of confidence on I, F and E components of NSQ respectively, but there was no significant improvement on An. component. This means certain degree of anxiety prevails in teacher-community.
8. During therapy males of experimental group improved more than their female counteparts. However, females were more submissive, obedient and dependent (E) than their male counterparts. And males were more sensitive and emotional (I) and slightly more serious (F) than females.
9. There was significant improvement in experimental group during pre-therapy to follow-up while in control group there was no improvement whatever. In follow-up experimental group became anxiety free while it was gripped by anxiety during therapy. This group improved (from .05 to .01 level of confidence) on E component also during this period. There was no change in control group during this period.
10. Cases 7, 10, 13, 14 and 17 achieved better adjustment after therapy and in follow-up, while cases 1, 5, 11, 12,

15, 18, 19, 20 and 22 become moderately adjusted during these periods.

C. SUGGESTIONS FOR FURTHER STUDY

In the light of the foregoing study the following suggestions are offered for further work as worthwhile :

1. This study may be replicated on a large sample of teachers and pupil-teachers in order to ensure superior validity for the findings and to assess the incidence of maladjustment.
2. In every teacher-training college there should be a cell for research on psycho-diagnosis and psycho-therapy for maladjusted trainees to enable them to be emotionally stable, so as to make them efficient and capable teachers.
3. Single-group design should be used in the study of maladjusted pupil-teachers so that all the identified maladjusted could be included in the study. If the number of these pupil-teachers is large, another researcher, who is acquainted with the psycho-therapy should be encouraged to study those problems. Alternatively all the maladjusted should be studied with moderately maladjusted in a parallel group design.
4. No-wait group should also be included in the study to compare its results with wait group. Hence experimental group should be divided into wait-group and No-wait-group (own-control group).
5. Attrition group should also be studied thoroughly.
6. Q-technique should also be used for assessing the improvement of adjustment as a handy alternative method.
7. Last but not the least, to test the comparative effectiveness of non-directive therapy, while using it (non-directive therapy) in treating one group, another method of therapy should be employed in treating the statistically equivalent group of maladjusted teachers-trainees.

D. IMPLICATIONS OF THE PRESENT STUDY

The present study has proved the methodology of therapy effective, hence, the non-directive approach of therapy should be used widely in rehabilitating the maladjusted teacher-trainees.

This study strongly indicates that better adjustment could be ensured amongst the pupil-teachers (who are prospective teachers) with the help of existing therapeutic resources in the teachers' training colleges, and thereby minimize mental health hazards of school children.

Thus there is good reason to believe that such effort will be conducive to education.

Bibliography

Ahuja. G.C. (1975), "Mental Health of Student-Teachers," *Teacher Education*, Vol, IX, No. 2, (January), pp. 34-56.

Altman, E. (1941), "Mentally Unbalanced Teachers," *Amer. Mercury*, 52, pp. 391-401.

Anderson, G.M. (1971), "Personality Characteristics of Aspiring Teachers and Experienced Teachers : A Discriminant Analysis," *Dissertation Abstracts International*, Vol. 31 (7-B), pp. 4323-24.

Anderson, H.H. and Brewer, H.M. (1945-46), "Studies on Teachers' Classroom Personalities," *Applied Psychology Monographs*, Nos. 6, 8 and 11.

Arnold, H. (1969), "A Study of Significance of Student-teachers' Personality Characteristics," *Journal of Teacher Education*, 20(2), pp. 143-47.

Barker, M.E. (1948), "Summary of the Relation of Personality Adjustments of Teachers to Their Efficiency in Teaching," *Journal of Educational Research*, 41, pp. 664-675.

Baxter, B. (1935), "An Objective Description of Teacher-Personality in Terms of Pupil-Teacher Behaviour." Unpublished Dissertation, Yale University.

Bentz, W. Kenneth, Hollister, William G. & Edgerton J.

Wilbert, (1971), "An Assessment of the Mental Health of the Teachers : A Comparative Analysis," *Psychology in the Schools*, 8, pp. 72-76.

Bernard, H. (1952), *Mental Hygiene for Classroom Teachers*, New York : McGraw-Hill Book Co.

Bina, K. (1964), "Personality and Intelligence of Student-Teachers." Unpublished Master's Thesis in Education, Agra University.

Boring, E.G. ; Langfeld, H.S. and Weld, H.P. (Eds.), (1951), *Foundations of Psychology*, New York : John Wiley and Sons, Inc., pp. 531 and 539.

Bowers, N.D. and Soar, Robert S. (1961), Studies of Human Relations in the Teaching-Learning Process, Part V : Final Report. USOE Cooperative Research Project No. 469, p. 210 in R.L. Ebel (1969), *Encyclopaedia of Educational Research*, Fourth Edition, London : Macmillan Co., p. 1430.

Bowman, Paul (1951), "A Study of the Consistency of Current, Wish, and Proper Self-concepts as a Measure of the Therapeutic Process." Unpublished Ph. D. Dissertation, University of Chicago.

Bown, Oliver (1954), "An Investigation of the Therapeutic Relationship in Client-Centred Psychotherapy". Unpublished Ph. D. Dissertation, University of Chicago.

Boynton, P.L., Dugger, H. and Turner, M. (1934), "The Emotional Stability of Teachers and Pupils." *Journal of Juvenile Research*, 18, p. 232.

Buch, M.B. (Ed.) (1979) *Second Survey of Research in Education*. Baroda : Society for Educational Research and Development, Chapter 7.

Burk, Donald D. (1970), "Personality Characteristics of Student-teachers and their Supervisors," *Dissertation Abstracts International*, Vol. 31 (3-A), p. 1111.

Butler, J.M. and Haigh, G.V. (1954), "Changes in the Relation between self-concepts and Ideal concepts consequent upon Client-Centered counselling," in C.R. Rogers and R.F. Dymond (Eds.) *Psychotherapy and Personality Change ; Coordinated Research Studies in the Client-Centred Approach* Chicago : The University of Chicago Press.

Carmichael, L. (1947), Editor's Introduction, in W.U. Snyder, *Casebook of Non-directive Counselling.* Boston : Houghton Mifflin Company.

Cattell, R.B. (1957), *Personality and Motivation Structure and Measurement.* New York : World Book.

—— and Eber, H.W. (1957), *Handbook for the Sixteen Personality Factor Questionnaire.* Illinois : The Institute for Personality and Ability Testing.

—— and Scheier, I.H. (1958), "The Nature of Anxiety : A Review of Thirteen Multivariate Analyses Comprising 814 variables, *Psychol. Rept.*, 4, pp. 351-388.

—— and Scheier, I.H. (1961), *The Meaning and Measurement of Neuroticism and Anxiety.* New York : Ronald Press.

—— and Stice, G.F. (1957), *Handbook for the 16 Personality Factor Questionnaire* (The 16 PF). Champaign, Illinois: The Institute for Personality and Ability Testing.

Chaplin, James P. (1968), *Systems and Theories of Psychology.* New York : Krawiec, Holt, Rinehart & Winston, Inc., p. 594:

Clark, E.J. (1950), The Mental Health of Elementary School Teachers as measured by the Guilford—Martin Personality Battery, *Teach. Coll. J.*, 22, pp. 27-28.

Coleman, James C. (1964), *Abnormal Psychology and Modern Life.* Bombay : D.B. Taraporevala Sons & Co., p. 14.

Crow Lester D. and Crow Alice (1951), *Human Development and Learning*, New York : American Book Co., p. 238.

Crow Lester D. and Crow, Alicee (1956), Human Development and Learning, New York : American Book Company, in C.E. Skinner (1958), *Elements of Educational Psychology*, p. 422.

Davies Lillian S. (1961), "Some Relationships between Attitude, Personality Characteristics and Verbal Behaviour of Selected Teachers," Doctoral Dissertation, University of Minnesota, p. 225, in R.L. Ebel, Ed. (1969), *Encyclopaedia of Educational Research*, Forth Edition, London ; Macmillan Company.

Dymond, R.F. (1954), "Adjustment Changes Over Therapy from Self-sorts," in C.R. Rogers and R.F. Dymond (Eds.) *Psychotherapy and Personality Change* : Coordinated

Research Studies in the Client-Centred Approach. Chicago : The University of Chicago Press.

Eysenck, H.J. *et. al.* (Ed.) (1975), Encyclopedia of Psychology, Fontana : Collins-Search Press, pp. 849-50.

Felix, Robert H. (1955), in *School Psychologists at Mid-Century*, Washington D.C. : American Psychological Association.

Fenton, N. (1943), *Mental Hygiene in School Practice.* Stanford : Stanford University Press, p. 289.

Fox, Margaret (1951), "A Quantitative Study of Changes in Verbal Behaviour occurring in Counselling." Unpublished Ph. D. Dissertation, University of Chicago.

Frierson, Marguerite S. (1950), "A Study of Mental Health Problems as they have related to turnover among 145 Elementary Teachers." Unpublished Ph. D Dissertation, Ohio State University.

Gallop, R. (1970), "A Study of the B. Ed. Students," *British Journal of Educational Psychology*, Vol. 40, Part I, p. 220.

Good, C.V. (1945), *Dictionary of Education*, New York : Mac Graw Hill Book Company, p. 392.

Gordon, T. and Cartwright, D.S. (1954), "The Effect of Psychotherapy Upon Certain Attitudes toward others" in C.R. Rogers and R.F. Dymond .(Eds.) *Psychotherapy and Personality Change.* Chicago : The University of Chicago Press.

Grummon, Donald L. (1950), "The Use of Language Categories for the Study of Personality and Psychotherapy," Unpublished Ph. D. Dissertation, University of Chicago.

—— (1954), "Personality Changes as a Function of Time in Persons motivated for Therapy," in C.R. Rogers and R.F. Dymond (eds.), *Psychotherapy and Personality Change.* Chicago : The University of Chicago Press.

——and John, E.S. (1954), "Changes Over Client-Centred Therapy Evaluated on Psycho-analytical based Thematic Appreciation Test Scales," in C.R. Rogers and R.F. Dymond (eds)., *Psychotherapy and Personality Change : Coordinated Research Studies in the Client Centred Approach.* Chicago : The University of Chicago Press.

Gupta. B.S. and Singhal, W.R. (1971) "Personality Adjustment Pattern of Pupil-teachers," *Journal of Education and Psychology*, Vol. xxiv, No, 3, pp. 230-233.

Hart, F.W. (1934), *Teachers and Teaching*, New York : The Macmillan Company.

Hartley, Margaret (1951), "Changes in the Self-Concept during Psychotherapy." Unpublished Ph. D. Dissertation, University of Chicago.

Hogan, Richard A. (1948), "The Development of a Measure of Client Defensiveness in the Counselling Relationship." Unpublished Ph. D. Dissertation, University of Chicago.

Jersild, A.T. (1963) "What teachers say about Psychotherapy." *Phi Delta Kappan*, 44, pp. 313-317.

Joneitz, Alice K. (1950), "A Study of the Phenomenological Changes in Perception after Psychotherapy as Exhibited in the Content of Rorschach percepts." Unpublished Ph. D. Dissertation, University of Chicago.

Kaplan, L. (1959), Mental Health and Human Relations in Education. New York : Harper & Row.

Kapoor, K. and Kapoor, S.D. (1974), Hindi Version of Scheier & Cattell's NSQ MMP Revised Hindi Edition, New Delhi : The Psycho-Centre.

Keliher, A.V. (1950), "Mental Hygiene in the Day's Work : A Day in the life of the Teacher." *Mental Hygiene*, 34, pp. 455-464.

Kell, Bill L. (1950), "An Experimental Study of the Ability to Predict the Self-Concept of an Individual from his Therapeutic Interview Behaviour." Unpublished Ph. D. Dissertation, University of Chicago.

Knapp, W.M. (1971), A Study of Teacher Personality Characteristics and Rated Effectiveness, *Dissertation Abstracts International*, Vol. 31, No. 11, p. 5712-A.

Laycock, S.R. (1950), "Effects of Teacher's Personality on the behaviour of Pupils," *Understanding the Child*, 19, pp. 50-55.

Lewin, K.R., Lippitt, and R.K. White (1939), "Patterns of Aggressive Behaviour in Experimentally Created 'Social Climates', *Journal of Social Psychology*, 10, pp. 271-299.

Mechane, George P. (1940), A Study of Emotional Stability of Teachers and their Pupils. Peabody College Contribution to Education in S.S. Mathur, *Educational Psychology*, Agra : Vinod Pustak Mandir, pp. 518-519.

Meehl, P.E. (1954), Clinical vs. Statistical Prediction, Minneapolis : University of Minnesota Press.

Mitchell, J.V. Jr. VI (1965), "Personality Characteristics associated with motives for entering teaching., *Phi Delta Kappan*, 46, pp. 529-232.

Mosak, Harold (1950), "Evaluation in Psychotherapy : A Study of Some Current Measures," Unpublished Ph. D. Dissertation, University of Chicago.

Negi, S.S. (1962), "A Survey of B. Ed. and L.T. Students of Lucknow City." Unpublished Master's Thesis in Education, Lucknow University.

Ottaway, A.K.C. (1951), "Mental Health in the Training of Teachers," *Bulletin of Education*, U.K. : Association of Teachers in Colleges and Departments of Education.

Parasher, V.N. (1961), "An Investigation into the Problems of Adjustment among the Pupil-teachers of B.T. Class." Unpublished Master Thesis in Education, Agra University.

Paul, S.K. (1968), "Personality Patterns of Engineering, Law Medical and Teacher-Training Students : A Comparative Study," *The Journal of Social Psychology*, 74, pp. 287-88.

Prasad, R.C and Singh, B.K. (1962), "Some Important Characteristics of Teachers and Students, "*Psychological Studies*, Vol. 7, pp. 23-31

Prasad, S.N. (1970), "Mental Illness as Social Deviance," *Indian Journal of Social Research*, Vol. XI, No. 2.

——(1972), "Education and Mental Health," *Samshiksha*, Faculty of Education, B.H.U., No. 2 April.

——(1972), "A Study of Relationships between Personality and Adjustment of Teacher-Trainees." Unpublished M.Ed. Disseratation, Banaras Hindu University.

——(1972), "Education as the Way to Ease the Stress," *Social Welfare* (New Delhi), Vol. XIX, No. 9, December.

——(1974), "Education and Mental Health for World," IAEWP Circulation Newsletter (U.S.A.), Vol. VI, No. 1.

Pressey, S.L., Robinson, F.P. and Horrocks (1967), *Psychology in Education* (Indian Edition), Delhi : Universal Book Stall, pp. 608-9.

Raina, T.N. (1968), "Authoritarianism of Indian Teacher Educators," *Journal of Teacher Education.* (Washington, D.C.).

——(1969), "An Application of F-scale to Indian Student-Teachers," *Indian Psychological Review*, Vol. 6, No. 1, p. 4.

Recommendation 36, (1953), Para 26, XVIth International Conference on Public Education, *Proceedings of Recommendation.* Paris : UNESCO.

Ringness, T.A. (1968), *Mental Health in the Schools*, New York : Random House, Inc., p. 42.

Rogers, Carl R. (1942), *Counselling and Psychotherapy*, New York : Grune and Stratton.

——(1944), "A Counselling Viewpoint for the USO Worker," *USO Programme Services Bulletin*, pp. 6-11.

——(1951) *Client-Centered Therapy.* Boston: Houghton Mifflin Company.

——(1954), "Changes in the Maturity of Behaviour as related to Therapy," in C.R. Rogers and R.F. Dymond (Eds.), *Psychotherapy and Personality Change.* Chicago : The University of Chicago Press.

——(1959), "Towards a Theory of Creativity," in A.H. Anderson (Ed.), *Creativity and its Cultivation.* New York : Happer and Row Publishers, p. 79.

——(1961), *On Becoming a Person : A Client's View of Psychotherapy*, Boston : Houghton Mifflin Company.

——and Dymond, R.F. (Eds.), 1954, *Psychotherapy and Personality Changes : Coordinated Research Studied in the Client-Centred Approach*, Chicago : The University of Chicago Press.

Rudikoff, E.C. (1954), "A Comparative Study of the Changes in the Concepts of the Self, The Ordinary Person, and the Ideal in the eight Cases," in C.R. Rogers and R.F. Dymond (Eds.), *Psychotherapy and Personality Change* : Chicago : Press.

Sarangi, T. (1963), "A Study of Personality and Attitude of Pupil-teachers in the State of Orissa." Unpublished Master's Thesis in Education, Utkal University.

Saxena, G, (1957), "Adjustment of Pupil-teachers at Vidya

Bhavan Teachers College, Udaipur." Unpublished Master's Thesis in Education, Rajasthan University.

Scheier, I.H. & Cattell, R.B. (1961), *Handbook for the Neuroticism Scale Questionnaire (The NSQ)*, Illinois: The Institute for Personality and Ability Testing, p. 4.

Shaffer, L.F. (1951) "Personal Adjustment" in E.G., Boring, H.S. Longfelds H.P. Weld, Foundations of Psychology, New York John wlly sons.

Sharma, K.L. (1963), "To Standardize a Test for Measuring Personality Traits of the Teachers to be selected for Primary Schools." Unpublished Master's Thesis in Education, Saugar University.

Sherman, M. and Jost, H. (1942), Frustration Reactions of Normal and Neurotic Persons", *Journal of Psychology*, 12, pp. 3-19.

Shipley, J.T. (1961), *The Mentally Disturbed Teacher*, Philadelphia : Chilton.

Skinner, Charles E. (Ed.) (1958), *Essentials of Educational Psychology*, N.J. : Prentice Hall, p. 421.

Smith, H.L. and Hightower, Jr. N.C. (1948), "Incidence of Functional Disease (Neurosis among Patients of various Occupations)" *Occupational Medicine*, 5, pp. 182-85.

Snyder, William U. (1945), "An Investigation of the Nature of Non-directive Psychotherapy," *Journal of General Psychology*, Vol. 33, pp. 193-223.

——(1947), "Do teachers cause maladjustment ?" *Journal of Exceptional Child*, 14, pp. 40-46.

——(1947), *Casebook of Non-directive Counselling*, Boston : Houghton Mifflin Company.

Soar, Robert S. (1966), "Research in the Teaching Processes : Four Studies with the OSCAR Technique," National Society of Colleges for Teacher Education, in R.L. Ebel, *Encyclopaedia of Educational Research*, Fourth Edition, London : Macmillan Company, p. 1430.

Swainson, M. (1952), "The Training of Teachers and their Mental Health," *New Era*, Vol. 33, No. 10 (Dec.).

Symonds, Percival M. (1949), "Education and Psychotherapy," *Journal of Educational Psychology*, Jan. 10, pp. 5-20.

——(1954), "Teaching as a function of the Teacher's Personality," *J. Teach. Educ.*, 5, 79-83.

——(1955), "Characteristics of the effective teachers based on pupil evaluation," *Journal of Experimental Education*, 23, pp. 289-310.

Tarpey, S.M.S. (1965), "Personality Factors in Teacher Trainee Selection," *British Journal of Educational Psychology*, Vol. XXXV, Part 2, pp. 140-49.

Thompson, Michael L. (1963), Identifying anxieties experienced by student teachers. *Journal of Teacher Education*, 14, pp. 433-449.

Townsend, M. (1933), Mental Hygiene and Teacher Recruiting, *Mental Hygiene*, 17, pp. 598-604.

Tyson, R. (1951), Occupational Hazards of Teaching : Working On Nerve, *Journal of Education*, pp. 134-26.

UNESCO Institute for Education (1955), *Report of an Expert Committee on Psychological Services for Schools and other Educational Institutions*, Section III. Hamburg : UNESCO Institute for Education.

Wall, W.D. (1955), *Education and Mental Health*, Paris : UNESCO.

Yourglich, A., (1955), "Study on Correlations between College Teachers and Students concept of Ideal student and Ideal Teacher," *Journal of Educational Research*, 49, pp. 59-64.

APPENDICES

APPENDIX I

गपयोनी
(IPATS 1961
Editon)

NSQ

HINDI VERSION OF SHEIER & CATTELL'S N.S.Q.

MMP 1974 Revised Hindi Edition

Prepared by :

K. KAPOOR and S.D. KAPOOR

नाम……………………स्त्री/पुरुष आयु :…………………………
वर्ष आज की तारीख……………………………………स्कूल/कालेज/
अपना पता……………………कक्षा शिक्षा स्तर………………………
अपना व्यवसाय पेशा………………मासिक आय, रु० ……………

यह प्रश्नावली आपसे आपके दृष्टिकोण, अभिरुचि आदि के विषय में प्रश्न पूछती है, जैसे—आप क्या करते हैं ? अथवा, विभिन्न परिस्थितियों में आपको कैसा लगता (अनुभव होता) है ? एक ही परिस्थिति में एक आदमी को एक प्रकार का अनुभव होता है तो दूसरे व्यक्ति को दूसरी ही तरह का अनुभव हो सकता है। इन प्रश्नों का कोई भी उत्तर पूर्वनिश्चित् "सही" या "गलत" नहीं है। अपने बारे में आप जैसा सोचते हैं या समझते हैं, केवल वही उत्तर सही और ठीक है।

अभ्यास के लिए नीचे दिये हुये तीन उदाहरणों से आप स्वयं समझ जायेंगे, जिसे आप मन में पढ़िये।

१. मुझे तैरने के लिए जाना पसन्द है।	हाँ ☐	अ ☐	नहीं ☐
२. मैं शाम का समय ज्यादातर इस तरह बिताना चाहूंगा। (क) लोगों के साथ बातचीत (गपशप) करने में, (ग) सिनेमा देखनें में।	क ☐	अ ☐	ग ☐
३. मुझे तमाशा देखनें के लिये घर से बाहर जाना पसन्द है।	क ☐	ख ☐	ग ☐

(क) बहुत कम, (ख) सामान्य रूप से;
(ग) हमेशा ।

जैसा कि आप देखते हैं कि हरेक प्रश्न किसी एक वाक्य के रूप में है और प्रश्न के तीन संभावित उत्तर दिये गये हैं : "हाँ", अनिश्चित ('अ'), "नहीं"; तथा क, अ, ग और क, ख, ग । आपको उत्तर देते समय कुछ लिखना नहीं है; केवल प्रश्नों को पढ़कर हरेक प्रश्न के सामने दिये खानों में से एक खाने (Box) में एक गुणा या क्रास का निशान बनाना है ।

ज्यादातर अवस्थाओं में आपका उत्तर "हाँ" (क) और "नहीं" (ग) में होना चाहिए । "हाँ" और "क" हमेशा बायीं ओर तथा "नहीं" और "ग" हमेंशा दायीं ओर मिलेंगे । **बीच के खाने (अनिश्चत "अ" या "ख") में आपको तभी निशान लगाना है जब आपके लिये किनारे के खानों द्वारा अपना उतर व्यक्त करना बिल्कुल असम्भव हो जाय !**

अब ऊपर लिखे हुये उदाहरण फिर से पढ़िये, और सामने दिये खानों में से किसी एक में अपने उत्तर को, जो भी आपको उचित जान पड़े, एक क्रास (×) का निशान Box के अन्दर लगाकर भर दें ।

अब :

(१) आप अच्छी तरह जाँच लीजिए कि आपने अपना नाम तथा अन्य बातें जो आपसे प्रारम्भ में पूछी गयी हैं, लिख दी हैं ।
(२) किसी भी प्रश्न को मत छोड़िये, बल्कि हरेक प्रश्न का कुछ न कुछ उत्तर अवश्य दें । अपने मन की बातें साफ-साफ कहिए, आपके उत्तर गुप्त रखे जायेंगें ।
(३) बहुत अधिक सोच-विचार में मत पड़िये, बल्कि तुरन्त मन में आये हुए विचारों को ही अपने उत्तर द्वारा भर दीजिये (पिछले सप्ताह के अथवा अपने रोज के विचारों को नहीं), भले ही आप इस तरह के प्रश्नों को पहले भी हल कर चुके हों फिर भी आप इस समय जैसा भी अनुभव करते हैं ठीक वैसा ही व्यक्त करें ।

साधारणतया कोई दस-बारह मिनट में अधिकतर लोग उत्तर दे देते हैं । इसे समाप्त करने पर ज्योंही आपसे कहा जाय इस प्रश्नावली को परीक्षक को लौटा दीजिये । संकेत मिलते ही पन्ना उलटिये और प्रारम्भ कीजिए ।

रुके रहिये— संकेत की प्रतीक्षा कीजिए

अपने उत्तर के लिए केवल खानों में ही निशान बनाइये ।

प्रत्येक प्रश्न के लिए केवल एक ही खाने में निशान बनाइये ।

अपने उत्तर नीचे दें

	क	ख	ग
१. स्कूल में मुझे सबसे अधिक यह पसन्द थी ,	☐	☐	☐
(क) हिन्दी (या अपनी मातृभाषा),	क	अ	ग
(ख) अंकगणित या गणित ।	☐	☐	☐
२. मुझे हर समय किसी कठिन शारीरिक	हाँ	अ	नहीं
काम में लगे रहना सचमुच ही पसन्द है ।	☐	☐	☐
३. किसी सिनेमा या सरकस में मुझे और चीजों के बजाय जोकर का रोल (या	हां	अ	नहीं
अभिनय) देखकर बेहद आनंद आता है :	☐	☐	☐
४. मैं इसे पढ़ना अधिक पसन्द करूंगा : (क) जिसमें फौजी लड़ाइयों का आँखों देखा हाल हो; (ग) एक मनगढन्त लेकिन मन के छू	क	अ	ग
लेने वाला उपन्यास ।	☐	☐	☐
५. बातचीत करते समय यदि कोई बीच में मुझे टोक देता है तो मैं अपनी बातचीत का विषय ही भूल जाता हूं , (क) हाँ, अक्सर; (ख) कभी-कभी;	क	ख	ग
(ग) शायद ही कभी ।	☐	☐	☐
६. मैं शाम का समय इस प्रकार बिताने में अधिक आनंद लेता हूं , (क) अपने मित्रों के साथ एक रोचक पार्टी में;	क	अ	ग
(ग) केवल अपने किसी शौकिया काम में ।	☐	☐	☐

७. मैं इस तरह से कपड़ा पहनना पसंद करता हूं :

(क) शान्ति से, और सही तरीके से;
(ख) आम तरीके से;
(ग) दूसरों का ध्यान आकर्षित करने के लिए कुछ खास तरीके से। क ☐ ख ☐ ग ☐

८. मैं सिनेमा या मन बहलाव के लिए घर से बाहर निकलना इतनी बार पसंद करता हूं :
(क) हफ्ते में एक बार से भी कम (आम लोगों से कम);
(ख) हफ्ते में लगभग एक बार (आम लोगों की तरह);
(ग) हफ्ते में एक बार से भी अधिक (आम लोगों से अधिक)। क ☐ ख ☐ ग ☐

९. मैं बिना झिझके साफ झूठ बोल सकता हूं
(क) जब कभी भी ऐसा करना ठीक हो;
(ख) कुछ दिक्कत से;
(ग) किसी भी दशा में, कभी भी नहीं। क ☐ ख ☐ ग ☐

१०. मैं लोगों से हंसी-मजाक करना बहुत अधिक पसंद करता। हां ☐ अ ☐ नहीं ☐

११. किसी समूह (ग्रुप) को क्या करना है, जब मैं इसे अच्छी तरह जान लेता हूं, तो स्वाभाविक रूप से उस समूह का शासन अपने हाथ में ले लेना मुझे पसंद है। हाँ ☐ अ ☐ नही ☐

१२. अपने खाली समय में, मैं अधिकतर इसमें शामिल होना चाहूंगा :
(क) पहाड़ की चोटी की खोज या उसे जीतने वाली टोली में;

(ग) किसी सामूहिक सेवा संगठन (Community Service Organisation) में। — क ☐ अ ☐ ग ☐

१३. मैं अपने बारे में नम्र होना ही ठीक समझता हूं, और जब लोग मुझसे किन्हीं मामलों में मेरी अच्छाइयों के बारे में पूछते हैं तो मैं उसे कुछ कम करके ही बतलाने में विश्वास करता हूं। — हाँ ☐ अ ☐ नहीं ☐

१४. यदि मैं यह समझता हूं कि बातचीत में कोई व्यक्ति गलती पर है तो मैं उसे साफ-साफ बता देता हूं
(क) केवल तभी जब यह भलमनसाहत से बताया जा सके; (ख) कभी-कभी;
(ग) हमेशा ही। — क ☐ ख ☐ ग ☐

१५. मुझे गन्दे और बेतुके शब्दों के प्रयोग से, नफरत होती है। — हाँ ☐ अ ☐ नहीं ☐

१६. मुझे अपने सारे माल-असबाव को किसी नई जगह पर ले जाने में बड़ी परेशानी मालूम पड़ती है। — हाँ ☐ अ ☐ नहीं ☐

१७. मैं वेशक इसे सुनना ज्यादा पसन्द करुंगा :
(क) एक बेंड बाजा;
(ग) एक सामूहिक भजन-कीर्तन। — क ☐ अ ☐ ग ☐

१८; झुंझलाहट की हालत में, मैं ऐसी बातें भी कर सकता हूं जो लोगों को चुभ जाती हैं :
(क) कभी नहीं; (ख) शायद ही कभी;
(ग) कभी-कभी। — क ☐ ख ☐ ग ☐

१९. सवेरे सोकर उठने पर अक्सर मुझे ऐसा लगता है कि मैं थका हुआ हूं। — हाँ ☐ अ ☐ नहीं ☐

२०. अपने काम में पूरा ध्यान देने में, मेरे लिए चीजों का बिल्कुल सही ढंग से सिलसिलेवार होना आवश्यक है। हाँ ☐ अ ☐ नहीं ☐

२१. मैं बेशक यह होना अधिक पसंद करूंगा :
(क) काम खोजने वाले नवयुवकों के भावी जीवन का सलाहकार (पथ-प्रदर्शक) होना,
(ग) किसी औद्यौगिक और उत्पादनशील व्यापारिक कम्पनी का मैनेजर होना। क ☐ अ ☐ ग ☐

२२. स्कूल में मुझे सबसे ज्यादा ये पसंद थी,
(क) दस्तकारी (या हाथ का काम),
(ख) हरेक समान रूप से; (ग) संगीत। क ☐ ख ☐ ग ☐

२३. दोपहर में मैं अपना खाली समय इस प्रकार बिताना ज्यादा पसंद करूंगा :
(क) ताश खेलकर;
(ग) किसी कला भवन में जाकर। क ☐ अ ☐ ग ☐

२४. मुझे समाचार-पत्र (अखबार) में निम्न-लिखित शीर्षकों में से, इसको पढ़ने में ज्यादा दिलचस्पी होगी :
(क) "उत्पादन और बाजार की आर्थिक दशा में नये सुधार";
(ग) "सब धर्मों के मेल पर धार्मिक नेताओं द्वारा बातचीत"। क ☐ अ ☐ ग ☐

२५. मैं सोचता हूं कि अधिकाँश लोगों के बजाय मैं अपने आसपास के वातावरण के कलात्मक गुणों के प्रति अधिक भावुक हूं। हाँ ☐ अ ☐ नहीं ☐

२६. मुझ में एक प्रवृति (आदत) एसा होने की है;

(क) एक बेहद आशावादी होने की (जो होगा सब अच्छा ही होगा);
(ग) एक बेहद सतर्क निराशावादी होने की (जो कुछ होगा बुरा ही होगा)। क ☐ अ ☐ ग ☐

२७. मेरे लिए सारा काम छोड़कर आराम करना एक बड़ा ही मुश्किल काम है। हाँ ☐ अ ☐ नहीं ☐

२८. मुझे हंसी-दिल्लगी करना और मजाकिया कहानी सुनना पसन्द है :
(क) शायद ही कभी; (ख) कभी-कभी;
(ग) अक्सर। क ☐ ख ☐ ग ☐

२९. मुझे बेशक इसमें अधिक दिलचस्पी होगी ;
(क) एक हंसमुख अभिनेता (ऐक्टर) बनने में;
(ग) गम्भीरतापूर्वक मकान को सही ढंग से सजाने में। क ☐ अ ☐ ग ☐

३०. भावनाओं या जज्बातों में बहक कर उसी समय काम करने में मुझे आनंद आता है (भले ही इनके कारण आगे चलकर मुझे कभी-कभी परेशानी ही क्यों न हो)। हाँ ☐ अ ☐ नहीं ☐

३१. मैं समझता हूं कि मेरे लिए यह ज्यादा जरूरी है कि :
(क) जो मैं सोचूं उसे ही करूं;
(ग) दूसरों के साथ मिल-जुलकर रहूं। क ☐ अ ☐ ग ☐

३२. जब मुझे अपने दोस्त की किसी ऐसी चीज को फौरन काम में लाने की जरूरत पड़ती है तो उसकी गैरमौजूदगी के बावजूद भी मैं उससे बिना पूछे ही उस चीज को ले लेना ठीक समझता हूं। हाँ ☐ अ ☐ नहीं ☐

३३. मेरे लिए यह अधिक जरूरी है कि मैं ; (क) अपने जीवन का अपने ही ढंग से शान्तिपूर्वक आनंद उठाऊं; (ग) अपने किये हुए कार्यों के लिए प्रशंसित एवं सम्मानित किया जाऊं ।	क ☐	अ ☐	ग ☐
३४. यदि मेरे हाथ में एक भरी हुई बन्दूक हो तो मुझे तब तक डर लगता रहेगा जब तक उसे खाली न कर दिया जाय ।	हाँ ☐	अ ☐	नहीं ☐
३५. मामूली जान-पहचान के लोगों से मैं मदद माँगने की कभी भी कोशिश नहीं करता ।	हाँ ☐	अ ☐	नहीं ☐
३६. कभी-कभी मुझे छोटी-छोटी बातों से बहुत ज्यादा घबराहट हो जाती है ।	हाँ ☐	अ ☐	नहीं ☐
३७. चिन्ता या बेचैनी के कारण मैं रात भर जागता रहता हूं : (क) कभी नहीं; (ख) कभी-कभी; (ग) अक्सर ।	क ☐	ख ☐	ग ☐
३८. मुझे ऐसा लगता है कि मैं जीवन में पूर्ण व्यवस्थित हूं और इसकी जरूरतों को अच्छी तरह निभा रहा हूं : (क) हमेशा; (ख) ज्यादा; (ग) बहुत कम ।	क ☐	ख ☐	ग ☐
३९. मुझे लगता है कि मेरे अच्छे इरादों की तुलना में लोग मेरे बारे में ज्यादा लिहाज नहीं रखते ।	हाँ ☐	अ ☐	नहीं ☐
४०. रोजमर्रा की घटनाओं पर जब मैं सोचता हूं तो कभी-कभी मैं बेचैन और अस्थिर हो उठता हूं ।	हाँ ☐	अ ☐	नहीं ☐

FOR EXAMINER'S USE

NSQ RECORD SHEET

Name ______________ Sex ____ Age ____ Date ________ Examiner ______________

Other Data

	TOTAL	ANALYSIS INTO COMPONENTS			
		SenIsit	DeFpr.	SubEmiss	An
Raw Score					
Sten Score					
PROFILE IN STENS — High 10					
9					
8					
7					
Average Range 6					
5					
4					
3					
2					
Low 1					
	TOTAL	Toulgh.	ChFeer.	Do Emn.	Not An.

Comments

Recommendations.

NSQ RECORD SHEET

APPENDIX II

Programme for the Calculation of SE_D by the formulas :

$$SD = \sqrt{\frac{SD_1^2 \times (N_1-1) - SD_2^2(N_2-1)}{(N_1-1)+(N_2-1)}}$$

$$SE_D = SD\sqrt{\frac{N_1+N_2}{N_1 \times D_2}}$$

Programme :

Step	Key	Step	Key
00	R/S	18	7
01	RCL	19	RCL
02	4	20	2
03	+	21	X
04	RCL	22	=
05	5	23	X
06	=	24	RCL
07	STO	25	5
08	6	26	=
09	RCL	27	÷
10	0	28	RCL
11	X	29	7
12	=	30	+
13	X	31	RCL
14	RCL	32	6

Step	Key	Step	Key
15	4	33	=
16	=	34	$\sqrt{\ }$
17	STO	35	STO
36	8	57	RCL
37	RCL	58	8
38	1	59	=
39	X	60	R/S
40	RCL	61	GO TO
41	3	62	0
42	=	63	0

Step	Key
43	STO
44	9
45	RCL
46	1
47	+
48	RCL
49	3
50	=
51	+
52	RCL
53	9
54	=
55	$\sqrt{\ }$
56	X

After feeding the programme and bringing the machine in run position, store the following values in the respective memories :

SD_1 in M_0
N_1 in M_1
SD_2 in M_2
N_j in N_3
(N_1-1) in M_4
(N_2-1) in M_5

Press GO TO 00 and then R/S key to get the result. Repeat the process unless all the values of SE_D are obtained.

Programme for the Calculation of t-value by the formula :

$$t = \frac{M_1 - M_2}{SE_D}$$

Programme :

Step	Key	
00	R/S	(Value of M_1)
01	—	
02	R/S	(Value of M_2)
03	=	
04	+	
05	R/S	(Value of SE_D)
06	=	
07	GO TO	
08	0	
09	0	

After feeding the programme, bring the machine in the run position. Register the value of M_1 and press R/S key ; then register the value of M_2 and press R/S ; now register the value of SE_D and press R/S to get the value of t. Repeat the process unless all the t-values are obtained.

APPENDIX III

First Test Scores on NSQ

Scores of Male Maladjusted Pupil-Teachers

Sr. No.	COMPONENTS OF NSQ I	F	E	An	Total NSQ Scores
1	13	14	16	12	55
2	10	9	19	13	51
3	9	6	18	8	51
4	10	13	10	16	49
5	7	14	16	12	49
6	12	6	15	18	51
7	11	14	14	15	54
8	10	17	16	10	53
9	14	10	15	17	56
10	14	9	13	13	49
11	11	10	13	16	50
12	17	14	13	10	54
13	14	11	18	11	54
14	13	12	18	8	51
15	12	12	18	9	51
16	13	12	15	13	53
17	16	11	13	10	50
18	10	12	18	15	55
19	13	10	15	12	50
20	12	10	14	13	49
21	16	12	10	14	52
22	9	12	15	14	52
23	14	8	12	15	49
24	13	14	16	11	54
25	8	14	16	11	49
26	10	10	16	15	51
27	13	9	18	10	50
28	14	7	13	17	51

APPENDIX IV

First Test Scores on NSQ
Scores of Female Maladjusted Pupil-Teachers

Sr. No.	COMPONENTS OF NSQ I	F	E	An	Total NSQ Scores
1	14	10	15	12	51
2	14	10	17	10	51
3	13	9	11	17	50
4	13	15	15	10	53
5	15	12	15	15	57
6	14	16	12	18	60
7	16	11	17	12	56
8	16	10	19	11	56
9	15	13	13	11	56
10	15	7	13	15	50
10	13	15	18	15	61
12	10	12	16	13	51

APPENDIX V

Pre-Wait Test Scores on NSQ
Scores of Experimental (Therapy) Group

Case No.	Subject	COMPONENTS OF NSQ I	F	E	An	Total NSQ Scores
1	I.R.	13	14	16	12	55
2	S.B.	14	10	15	12	51
3	A.M.	10	9	19	13	51
4	G.B.	9	16	18	8	51
5	V.G.	10	13	10	16	49
6	M.S.	14	10	17	10	51
7	Y.T.	7	14	16	12	49
8	V.V.	12	6	15	18	51
9	D.D.	11	14	14	15	54
10	K.J.	13	9	11	17	50
11	R.H.	10	17	16	10	53
13	M.M.	14	10	15	17	56
13	H.H.	14	9	13	13	49
14	M.K.	11	10	13	16	50
15	R.N.	17	14	13	10	54
16	V.L.	14	11	18	11	54
17	A.L.	13	12	18	8	51
18	S.P.	13	15	15	10	53
19	M.N.	15	12	15	10	57
20	S.R.	14	16	12	18	60
21	S.S.	16	11	17	12	56
22	R.S.	16	10	19	11	56
23	S.K.	12	12	18	9	51

APPENDIX VI

Pre-Wait Test Scores on NSQ : Scores of Control (No-therapy) Group

Case No.	Subjects	Components of NSQ I	F	E	An	Total NSQ Scores
1	V.T.	13	12	15	13	53
2	D.R.	16	11	13	10	50
3	U.C.	10	12	18	15	55
4	S.B.C.	15	13	13	15	56
5	G.V.	13	10	15	12	50
6	S.P.K.	12	10	14	13	49
7	K.C.	16	12	10	14	52
8	R.M.	9	12	15	14	52
9	R.S.P.	14	8	12	15	49
10	B.M.	13	14	16	11	54
11	M.N.R.	8	14	16	11	49
12	K.N.	15	7	13	15	50
13	D.K.	10	10	16	15	51
14	N.V.	13	15	18	15	61
16	S.B.W.	13	9	18	10	50
16	T.D.	14	7	13	17	51
17	S.H.	10	15	16	13	51

APPENDIX VII

Before Therapy Test (Pre-test) Scores on NSQ
Scores of Experimental (Therapy) Group

Case No.	Components of NSQ				Total NSQ Scores
	I	F	E	An	
1	13	14	17	13	57
2	15	9	15	13	52
3	11	8	18	12	49
4	8	17	18	7	50
5	10	14	10	6	50
6	12	10	17	10	49
7	7	14	16	12	49
8	12	7	14	17	50
9	11	13	12	14	50
10	13	9	11	17	50
11	10	17	15	10	52
12	13	10	16	17	56
13	16	9	13	14	50
14	10	10	14	15	49
15	17	14	12	9	52
16	13	10	17	10	50
17	13	12	17	8	50
18	13	14	14	10	51
19	14	12	14	14	54
20	13	15	12	17	57
21	15	10	16	11	52
22	14	10	17	11	52
23	12	12	16	9	49

APPENDIX VIII

Before Therapy Test (Pre-test) Scores on NSQ
Scores of Control (No-therapy) Group

Case No.	Components of NSQ				Total NSQ Scores
	I	F	E	An	
1	13	12	15	14	54
2	16	11	13	11	51
3	10	12	18	16	56
4	15	13	13	14	55
5	13	10	15	13	51
6	12	10	14	13	49
7	16	12	10	14	52
8	9	12	15	14	52
9	14	8	12	15	49
10	13	14	16	11	54
11	8	14	16	11	49
12	15	7	13	15	50
13	10	10	16	15	51
14	13	15	18	15	61
15	13	9	18	10	50
16	14	7	13	17	51
17	10	12	16	13	51

APPENDIX IX

Post-Therapy Test (Post-test) Scores on NSQ Scores of Experimental (Continuers) Group

Sr. No. of cases From Ex. Group	Components of NSQ				Total NSQ Scores
	I	F	E	An	
1	10	12	15	11	48
5	14	6	12	10	42
7	10	11	11	6	38
10	8	8	10	15	41
11	10	8	12	15	45
12	8	13	13	13	47
13	13	9	9	11	41
14	13	9	9	5	36
15	8	11	14	11	44
17	8	8	11	13	40
18	7	11	17	7	42
19	11	9	14	13	47
20	8	11	16	14	48
22	14	7	12	11	44

APPENDIX X

Post-Therapy Test (Post-test) Scores on NSQ Scores of Control (No-therapy) Group

Sr. No. of cases from Con. Group	Components of NSQ				Total NSQ Scores
	I	F	E	An	
1	13	12	15	13	53
4	15	13	13	15	56
8	9	12	15	14	52
9	14	8	12	15	49
11	8	14	16	11	49
12	15	7	13	14	49
14	13	15	18	14	60
16	14	7	13	17	51
17	10	12	16	13	51

APPENDIX XI

Follow-np Test Scores on NSQ
Scores of Experimental Group

Sr. No of cases from Ex. Group	Components of NSQ				Total NSQ Scores
	I	F	E	An	
1	10	12	13	10	45
5	14	6	12	10	42
7	10	11	11	6	38
10	8	8	10	16	41
11	10	8	12	15	45
12	8	13	13	13	47
13	13	9	8	11	41
14	13	9	9	5	36
15	8	11	14	11	44
17	8	8	11	13	40
18	7	11	17	7	42
19	11	9	14	13	47
20	8	10	15	14	46
22	14	7	12	11	44

APPENDIX XII

Follow-Up Test Scores on NSQ
Scores of Control Group

Sr. No. of subjects from Con. Group	Components of NSQ				Total NSQ Scores
	I	F	E	An	
1	13	12	14	13	52
4	15	13	13	14	55
8	9	12	15	14	52
9	14	8	12	15	49
11	8	14	16	11	49
12	15	7	13	14	49
14	13	15	18	14	60
16	14	7	13	17	51
17	10	12	16	13	51

Index